The Way I Remember It

Tales from a Port St. Joe Childhood & Beyond

H. Higdon Swatts

The Way I Remember It

CONTENTS

DEDICATION

This book of short stories is dedicated to many good friends and teachers who have made a positive impact on my life. Also to those who have read some of my stories and encouraged me to publish them.

Thank you!

ACKNOWLEDGEMENTS

I may have written a few stories along the way that may or may not be worthy of being published, but I know that I would have never attempted to have them published into a book without the encouragement and expertise of my daughter, Dana Swatts Kerigan. This young lady has spent countless hours researching the requirements of the publisher and applying her newfound knowledge to the endeavor of bringing this book to the point of being published.

Of course, like her dad, Dana is a Florida native. She holds a Bachelor of Science degree from the Florida State University School of Business and is a Certified Purchasing Manager (C.P.M.). She and her husband, Jack, are the owners of Kerigan Marketing Associates, a full-service marketing agency, in Mexico Beach, Florida. She is active in the community and in her church, and loves spending time making memories with her family.

With a grateful heart, I hereby express my profound appreciation for all Dana has done to help bring this publication to fruition.

Special thanks also goes out to the following people who provided professional services that helped make this book a reality.

Sara Backus – *Creative Director / Book Cover Design*
Daron Adkins – *Photographer*
Todd Davidson – *Copywriter / Back Cover Copy*
Mollie Etheridge – *Communications / Photoshoot assistance*
Olivia Wesel – *Social Media / Photoshoot assistance*
Kerigan Marketing Associates, Inc. - *Publisher*

CHAPTER 1

A NICKEL IS BIGGER

When I was about six years old, I was always being teased by the other neighborhood boys for being stupid. Their favorite joke was to offer me my choice between a nickel or a dime. I always took the nickel because it was bigger than the dime.

SCHOOL DAYS 1950-51

PORT ST. JOE

One day, after I had taken the nickel, one of my best friends said to me, "Higdon, those boys are making fun of you. Don't you know that a dime is worth more than a nickel, even though the nickel is bigger?" I just grinned and said, "Well yeah, but if I took the dime, they'd stop offering it, and so far, I've made about $20."

1

CHAPTER 2

NO TIDAL WAVE
IN OLD ST. JOSEPH

For many years, stories have been told about how a Tidal Wave once destroyed old St. Joseph back in 1843.

According to my great grandfather, (James Bennett Stone) who, in the year 1843, was a resident of Old St. Joseph at the time reported that there was a huge storm with high winds, that blew down many trees, moved through westward and hung over the Gulf for a time and then reversed itself, blowing to the east and piling up water in St. Joseph Bay. The result caused an extremely high tide which inundated most of the area around Old St. Joseph. More than likely, this was what we would call today, a hurricane.

According to my grandfather, his father, James Bennett Stone was forced to move inward to an area about where Ward Ridge stands today. Reportedly, he climbed up into a stout tree and lashed himself to it with a rope to keep from drowning or being seriously injured.

There have been several books written by people who did not live in Old St. Joseph, that told of stories of a tidal wave that destroyed the city. According to my grandfather, no tidal wave ever hit Old St. Joseph. These stories were written and told for very distinct reasons.... mainly to keep St. Joseph from rebuilding to the possible detriment of newly developed nearby holdings in cities such as Apalachicola, Pensacola, Mobile and other gulf coast settlements.

Many of the old buildings were torn down for the salvage value they produced, while others were moved to Apalachicola where a number of them still stand today. According to my great grandfather, no buildings were demolished by a "tidal wave" as some stories relate.

As a bit of prior history, the settlement that had sprung up on beautiful St. Joseph's Bay, called St. Joseph, gradually had increased in size until it boasted an estimated 10,500 population, being the largest city in Florida at that time. As the city flourished, it soon became one of the largest seaports on the Gulf. A large shipyard was located on what is now the site of the Port Inn. Sometime after the constitutional convention was held in 1838, the city began to decline. There have also been reports of a large fire that also partially destroyed the city. I even though heard this myself growing up in Port St. Joe but I have never seen any written reports of a fire nor did my grandfather ever mention it to me.

Depopulated by a depression, which left no way for the inhabitants of St. Joseph to secure a livelihood and then the Yellow Fever Scourge that struck leaving thousands dead while others fled to avoid the fever. The Storm of 1843 pretty well finished off the old city, but it has been said that there was NO tidal wave.

CHAPTER 3

A FIDDLE &
A MARRIAGE PROPOSAL

In 1903, my grandfather (Terrell Higdon Stone) was a young man, and he lived in Iola, FL just northeast of Wewahitchka. He delivered the U.S. Mail by boat up and down the Chipola River. On Saturday nights, along with some of his friends, he would play his fiddle for local barn dances. Barn dances were very common in southern small-town communities and were sometimes the only means of entertainment the locals had.

On one particular moonlit night, when Granddaddy was on his way to play a gig, he walked past the Iola Hotel. As he passed by, he noticed a pretty young girl on the front porch, swinging in a porch swing. All he knew at the time was that the owners of the hotel had a niece who was visiting them for the summer. He tilted his hat and went along his way to the barn dance. The whole time he was playing for the dance, he couldn't get the young girl off his mind.

Sometime around 11:00 PM, the dance came to an end and

Granddaddy started his return trip home. A few minutes later, he had reached the hotel and noticed that the young girl was still swinging in that swing. As he approached, he made it a point to walk a little closer to the porch, and once again tilted his hat to the young maiden. As he walked on toward his home, he suddenly became convinced that the girl had waited up for him to make his return trip back by the hotel.

That night Granddaddy couldn't sleep and decided that the next morning, he would make it a point to call on the girl. Morning couldn't come soon enough and shortly after 8:00 AM, Granddaddy

nervously made his way to the hotel to eat breakfast at the hotel dining room. As luck would have it, the girl that he seen the night before, came over to his table to take his order. He soon introduced himself and quickly found out that her name was Annie Virginia

Wynn and that she was from Dublin, Georgia. She had been raised by another aunt and uncle from that fair city.

Now Granddaddy quickly made his move and asked if she would allow him to come calling. Of course, she said she would have to ask her aunt and uncle's permission. Soon, she returned to his table and related that it was fine with them as they had known him for some time as their Postman. Granddaddy called on Miss Annie for the remainder of the summer and by summers end had asked for her hand in marriage. Shortly after that, they were married.

In 1894, both of Granddaddy's parents had passed away and he had inherited a large track of land that ran for miles along the Gulf Coast from what is now Port St. Joe and extended south all the way out to Cape San Blas. In late 1903, he left his young wife behind in Iola and traveled south to begin a turpentine business.

By mid-1904, he had built a home suitable for he and his young wife and soon moved her to the area. Here, the two of them would begin a family and a community that would later be named Port St. Joe. There have been many stories that earned their way into the history of Port St. Joe; most of them were even true.

One picture shown in this chapter is of my granddaddy when he was young and the other is of the "fiddle" that he played for the barn dances. The difference between a fiddle and a violin is the person who plays them.

I still have that fiddle. Sometimes, at night I am awakened by what I would swear is the sound of a fiddle being played somewhere far off but once awake I can't hear it anymore. Can anyone give me an answer to that?

CHAPTER 4

THE FIRST CHURCH IN PORT ST. JOE

The first ever church in Port St. Joe was organized in 1912 in a little two-room school house. This school house most likely was also used for the first school. A Sunday School was organized by Mr. A.M. Jones Sr. and Mr. T.H. Stone, both early settlers of Port St. Joe. The Sunday School served all denominations, but all used Methodist literature. A little later the same group, again led by Mr. Jones and Mr. Stone, met in the lobby of the old Port Inn (long since burned) to organize the Methodist Church. The Reverend C. L. Middlebrooks, serving as Pastor of the Wewahitchka and Indian Pass churches, held a few services, but the first regular pastor of the church was the Reverend E. A. Childs. Except for the first few services held in the lobby of the Port Inn, the little school house was used until the first Methodist Church building was completed in 1914.

For many years, the Methodist Church served as the meeting place for Baptist, Presbyterian and Episcopal congregations and it was in this building that the other churches were officially organized.

This is the church that I attended with my family during the first eight years of my life until the present Methodist Church was built around 1949 and was officially dedicated in 1956. I was a member of the Church until 1984 when I joined Central Baptist Church in Panama City. I am presently a member of First Baptist Church of Panama City.

The picture below was taken of the first church in about 1946. The 1946 Ford parked in front belonged to Jim McNeil's faithful grandparents, Mr. & Mrs. J.T. McNeil, who lived at Indian Pass and hardly ever missed a service.

CHAPTER 5

PORT ST. JOE'S
FIRST FIRE ENGINE

When I was about ten years old, I used to spend a lot of time at my grandparents' home which was located where Hungry Howie's is now. In the back of the property was and old storage house crammed full of all sorts of junk. Now my grandfather (Terrell Higdon Stone) always told me to stay out of that old building because there might be snakes, spiders and other critters in there.

There were times when he would be gone and I, being curious, would climb through a window on the back side and crawl all over that junk. Granddaddy had been the city's first Postmaster as well as the second mayor and there were a lot of old postal boxes, desk and the Lord knows what else was stored in there.

One item that caught my attention was some old wagon wheels on a frame with some sort of tank mounted on it. Not knowing what it was made me curious, but I couldn't ask Granddaddy because he would know I had been in that building. It was a few years later that I found out that the mobile tank was the city's first fire engine. You may ask how come it's called a fire engine when there was clearly no engine attached. My answer to you would be that it's called that because there's a brass tag attached to the tank that clearly spells "Fire Engine".

It was called a Hand Drawn Fire Engine which meant a couple of firemen would manually pull it to the location of the fire. The tank would be filled with some sort of fire retardant mixed with water which would hopefully assist the firefighters in putting the fire out.

During the early 1970's, my grandparents' home was torn down and the man tearing it down also tore down the old storage building. He asked my Uncle Mickey (Stone) what he wanted him to do with the old fire apparatus. Uncle Mickey contacted the fire department and offered it to them to be saved as part of the department's history. The fire department graciously accepted and had someone restore the old engine and then placed it on display in the fire station where it remains today.

One day while I was in St. Joe, I asked my niece to meet me at the station to take pictures of it so that I could write this story about it. Some of you may not know, but the City of Port St. Joe was established as a city in 1913. The year 1913 is stenciled on the front of this old engine.

Now you know the "rest of the story" or as much of it as I know anyway.

CHAPTER 6

JUST PLAIN CHEAP

I remember when I was a small boy, my dad telling me a story about a businessman who owned a general store in my dad's home town of Whigham, Georgia. Now everyone in Whigham knew everybody else and they all knew the businessman whose name was Mr. John Tuttle and most everyone also knew how "tight" he was (Tight meaning: Tightwad or Conservative).

Now Mr. Tuttle had a 17-year-old son named John Jr. who attended high school at Whigham High. Every day after school, John Jr. would walk from the school to his dad's general store where he worked until dark thirty (closing time).

Mr. Tuttle, being a man of means, purchased a new 1918 Model T Ford to drive to and from home to work. Most of the town's

people were still using horse and buggies or wagons in those days.

Each night, after closing the store, Mr. John and John Jr. would load up in the Model T and head home. Gasoline at that time was about 10 cents a gallon and it just about killed Mr. John to have to buy gas for that Model T, being that he was so tight and everything.

The narrow two-rut road from town to Mr. Tuttle's home was about two miles from town. About half way along the way was a sloping hill that descended to a small creek which had a wooden bridge at the bottom. Just past the bridge, the narrow road began its incline back up to the top of the hill.

Now Mr. Tuttle, being the conservative man that he was, would put the transmission into neutral as he began to descend the hill, coasting all the way down to the bridge at the bottom and stop. He would then have John Jr., who weighed about two hundred pounds, get out of the car and walk up to the top of the hill on the other side, while Mr. Tuttle drove the car up to the top.

Neighbors who witnessed this asked Mr. Tuttle why he made the young boy walk up the hill and his reply was "Well the boy now weighs so much that it would take more gas for the car to climb that there hill and you know that there gas ain't cheap".

CHAPTER 7

FIRST CATHOLIC CHURCH IN PORT ST. JOE

Before St. Joseph's Catholic Church was established in Port St. Joe, Priests were brought from Apalachicola by rail in a 1910 Cadillac inspection car which was mounted on railroad wheels (See picture below).

The inspection car was chauffeured by Charles Mahon along the railroad tracks of the Apalachicola Northern Railroad Company from Apalachicola to Port St. Joe.

The name St. Joseph's Catholic Church should not be confused with the town of old St. Joseph of the 1800's. St. Joseph is the name of the present church which was first established in 1925.

In the early 1900's, Mass was celebrated in the home of Mr. & Mrs. Dennis Sullivan. In 1918, lots were purchased on Eighth

Street, with plans to build a church, but due to the small number of Catholics at that time, the building project was postponed.

In 1920, the Reverend Francis De Sales offered his first Mass in the home of Mr. & Mrs. Robert Tapper (George Tapper's parents). In 1925, the first Catholic Church, (see picture below) was built on Eighth Street and was dedicated by Bishop Allen. Charles Brown and Ida Ethel Kilbourne were the first couple to be married in that church.

On April 12, 1959, his Excellency Archbishop Toolen, dedicated the present St. Joseph's Catholic Church, which is located on the corner of 20th Street and Monument Avenue. This was a very special occasion for the members of this new church.

CHAPTER 8

From Port St. Joe to Panama City in a 1923 Model T Ford

In 1923, my grandfather, (Terrell Higdon Stone) ordered a new 1923 Model T Ford Touring Car from Ford Motor Company. In those days, Ford would ship their cars by rail to small cities like Port St. Joe if there was not a dealership. They would be shipped partly unassembled and would have to be put together by a mechanic. Once received, my grandfather paid to have someone assemble it.

Now Granddaddy only drove that Model T one time because he couldn't figure out how to get it to stop. He had put only one quart of gasoline in the gas tank, so he figured if he couldn't stop it, he would just drive it until it gave out of gas.

When it finally gave out of gas, he told my Uncle Nobie that he would just have to learn how to drive that contraption so that the family would have some sort of transportation besides a horse and buggy and that he was done with that "thing". Uncle Nobie, being the oldest child, learned very quickly and was soon seen sporting the Model T around the muddy two-rut roads of Port St. Joe.

Sometime later that year, Uncle Nobie talked Granddaddy into letting him make a trip to Panama City. The only way Granddaddy would agree to let him go, was if he would take all the kids (four others) with him and treat them to a movie and an overnight stay at the Panama City Hotel.

Uncle Nobie agreed and the trip was planned. All the other kids were excited. On the selected day, they all loaded up in the Model T with one change of clothes each and enough gas to get them to their destination. With Uncle Nobie driving, Uncle Mickey road up front and my mother, Aunt Ola and Uncle Jesse road in the back seat. Granddaddy had given Uncle Nobie enough money to pay for the trip, which included gas, the movie, food and the hotel rent. As they pulled away from the house, Mama Stone had come out on the front porch with Granddaddy to wave goodbye to their babies.

Once on the road, Uncle Nobie knew that he would have to navigate that two-rut sandy road all the way to Panama City, including crossing the bay between Redfish Point and Panama City on a ferry. The trip in the Model T was expected to take almost all day. Leaving very early, they hoped to get there by midafternoon in time to catch the movie.

As luck would have it, they reached their destination on time and Uncle Nobie pulled up in front of the theatre. He gave each child enough money for their ticket and enough for popcorn, candy and a drink. He told them he would be back to pick them up when the movie was over. He then drove on down the street to

Cook Motor Company which was the Ford dealership, where he went inside and purchased every available accessory that could be put on a Model T Ford and had them all installed. By the time this was completed, it was time to go back to the theatre to pick up his siblings.

As soon as everyone was on board, Uncle Nobie announced that they would be returning to Port St. Joe that night because he had spent all the hotel and food money on accessories for the Model T Ford. It was a long trip home that night and they finally arrived sometime just before dawn. What really made that trip home so long was that Uncle Nobie knew what was in store for him when he got there. I believe he drove pretty slow.

I never really heard what happened, but my imagination did double backflips while I was thinking about what might have happened.

CHAPTER 9

THE HISTORY OF ST. JOSEPH TELEPHONE & TELEGRAPH

St. Joseph Telephone & Telegraph Company was first established in 1924 by Apalachicola Northern Railroad Company. Prior to that time the railroad company had a small switchboard which supplied limited telephone service to some of its key employees. A telegraph line had been built from Port St. Joe to Chattahoochee which gave the company telegraph service to railroad depots located in St. Joe, Apalachicola, Sumatra, Telogia and Chattahoochee. When the DuPont's purchased land in 1935 to build St. Joe Paper Company, they also acquired the Railroad Company and along with it, the Telephone Company.

St. Joseph Telephone & Telegraph Company became one of the most progressive telephone companies in the State of Florida. It was the first company to change all its exchanges over to dial systems in the 1950's. It later became the first in the state to completely change over all exchanges to one party service. Another first for the State was the fact that the company was the first to change over all its exchanges to Touch-Tone Dialing. Lastly, it was the first company in the State to completely change all its exchanges over to Digital Telephone Switches.

My tenure with St. Joseph Telephone & Telegraph Company began in June of 1962 and ended in retirement 35 years later in

1997. In 1996, the company was sold and has been sold two additional times since. I was proud have been with the company during the years of so many changes which led to better service for its subscribers.

CHAPTER 10

SELECTING A NAME FOR A NEW COUNTY

Back in the early 1920's, my grandfather, T. H. Stone, served as a county commissioner for Calhoun County. To attend commission meetings once a month, he would ride his mule from Port St. Joe to Abe Springs, which was the county seat of Calhoun County. This was a two-day trip.

After trying for several years, my grandfather with the help of many others, finally was able to get a bill passed through state legislation, dividing Calhoun County into two parts. This was accomplished in 1925.

After the county was divided, an election was held, and new commissioners were elected for the newly formed county. At the first county commission meeting, the first order of business was to name the new county. One of the commissioners made a motion to name the county Satsuma County.

At that time, my grandfather spoke up and said, "Wait a minute, I know that we have many satsuma trees in this area, but we could have a hard freeze and lose most of the trees in one season. Why don't we name the county Gulf County, because there will always be a Gulf out there?" The commissioners voted, and the rest is history. (Gulf County History, that is.)

CHAPTER 11

THE MISS STEPPIE & THE LOW MAINTENANCE BUOY

I must have been about 10 years old when one day I was wading in the bay close to the city pier. I was about knee deep in the water when I stepped on a solid object. I reached down into the water and pulled up a wooden plank about three (3) feet long. The plank had at once time been painted white and had a couple of words painted on it. You could barely make it out, but it spelled Miss Step. At the end of the letter p, the board was broken off and jagged. Not knowing where it might have come from, it didn't seem to matter, so I just dropped it back into the water.

When I got home that day, I told my mother about the board that I had found. She said, "That's part of your granddaddy's old boat named Miss Steppie." She then explained that Granddaddy had a boat for many years that was about 35 to 40 feet long, that he used to use in his turpentine business. He would haul turpentine down the canal and into the bay, where he off-loaded it on to rail cars which were spotted on the AN Railroad loading dock that went out into the water. The loading dock was also used by the lumber company to ship their lumber on ocean going vessels to other ports on the Gulf. Granddaddy also used his boat to carry Navel stores to Pensacola. The next day I went back down to the bay to look for that Miss Steppie board, but never could find it.

I so wish that I had never thrown it back. I would love to still have it today.

Mother said that Granddaddy had quit using the boat in about 1938 and had moored it in the bay about 100 feet from the shoreline, pretty much even with the corner of Eight Street & Highway 98. Sometime in the early 1940's, Miss Steppie was destroyed by a hurricane. All that was left of it was the old engine boiler. The wheelhouse part of the boat ended up on the bayside beach close to the end of Cape San Blas.

The "Miss Steppie" which carried Naval stores to Pensacola.

Mother told me that Granddaddy at one time was able to jack up the boiler and put some wagon wheels under it with the hope of removing it from the bay. She said that he had hitched up a couple of mules to it, trying to pull it out, but to no avail. My brother and I waded out to the boiler one time and dove down to verify that those wheels were still there. They were.

Over the years, the old boiler has been used as a buoy, marking a natural channel that runs just beyond the city pier and parallel to the beach for several hundred yards. On low tide, it is possible to run aground if you don't follow this channel. My guess is that very few people in this area have ever known the true history of this object in the bay. It might just be the only maintenance free buoy in the bay and it is still there today, but I bet it's not on the Coast Guard's Charts.

Now you know about Miss Steppie and the maintenance free buoy.

CHAPTER 12

NO BANK ON REID AVE

Back in 1903, My grandfather, T.H. Stone, made his way from the Stone Mill Creek area down to what is now named Port St. Joe. During those days it was known as Indian Pass. He came to the area to establish a turpentine business. Years before this, his father, James Bennett Stone, had purchased tax deeds on the land which spanned from Beacon Hill to Dead Man's Curve, including Cape San Blas on the south end and to almost White City to the North. This area was all located in Calhoun County at the time and when James Bennett died in 1894, the land was willed to my grandfather.

As there was no inhabitant in the area, one the first things Granddaddy did when he arrived in 1903, was to build a small log cabin to live in while building a larger house for his new bride. The small log cabin was located in the area of what is now 6th Street and Reid Avenue, in Port St. Joe.

Now, fast forward to the early 1930's, a man by the name of Alfred I. du Pont came to the area and purchased large tracks of timberland from my grandfather. Also included in this sale was the land along St. Joseph's Bay from about where the Highland View Bridge is located, running south to about where Capital City Bank is located today. Mr. DuPont announced plans to build a paper mill on this land, which was to be named St. Joe Paper Company. Mr. du Pont died in 1935 leaving an estate in banks, land and securities worth $58 million. Dupont's brother-in-law, Edward Ball was soon selected to manage the estate, which included the construction of the paper mill in Port St. Joe.

Soon after the construction of the mill began, my grandfather decided that he wanted to move his old log cabin down close to the bay, so he contacted Mr. Ball and made a request to re-purchase one acre of land somewhere close to what is now Frank Pate Park. Mr. Ball replied that he was in the business of purchasing land and not selling it. This, needless to say, did not set well with my granddaddy. He vowed never to sell any more land to the DuPont's.

Sometime in about 1938, I believe, Mr. Ball decided to build a bank in Port St. Joe and he contacted Granddaddy about the possibility of purchasing a corner lot on 4th Street & Reid Avenue to build the bank. Granddaddy told Mr. Ball that if he built a bank in Port St. Joe, that he would have to build it on property already owned by the company and that he would not sell any more land to DuPont. The nearest downtown property owned by the company was on the corner of what is now Cecil G. Costin Blvd and Long Avenue. The Florida National Bank of Port St. Joe, was built on this property and opened for business on February 1, 1940 and remained at this location until a new Florida National Bank building was built in 1965 at 504 Monument Avenue.

And that, my friends, is the reason that the first bank of Port St. Joe was not built downtown on Reid Avenue. My grandfather did his banking with Apalachicola State Bank in Apalachicola.

CHAPTER 13

T.H. STONE &
THE PORT THEATRE

During the time when the Paper Mill was being built, Mr. Martin, who owned several movie theatres in the area, drove down to Port St. Joe to look for property to build a theatre. When he arrived, he asked someone who owned property on Reid Avenue and was told that would be Higdon Stone. Well, it didn't take him long to find Mr. Stone, and when he did, he asked about the possibility of purchasing a site suitable for a theatre.

The site was selected and the two of them came to an agreement on price and then there was a gentlemen's handshake, which was common in those days between businessmen before paperwork was signed. Mr. Martin said that he would be back in a couple of weeks to finalize the deal. Mr. Stone said that would be fine, and that during that time he would prepare the deed. Mr. Martin also commented that he was just finishing a theatre in Panama City and had some brick and steel left over and wanted to know if he could ship those materials on down to St. Joe and store them on the property. Mr. Stone agreed to this request.

The next week Mr. Martin sent a crew down with the materials. The young man who was in charge, asked someone where he could find Mr. Stone and soon approached Mr. Stone at his home. The young man, thinking that he might get into good graces with Mr. Martin, began to tell Mr. Stone that he had looked at the property and that he thought the price was too high. Mr. Stone told the young man that the price had already been agreed on and that he and Mr. Martin had shaken hands on the deal.

At this time, the young man said that he would just look around for other available property on Reid Avenue. Mr. Stone told him that he owned all the available property and if he insisted on changing the terms of the agreement, then the deal was off. The young man, thinking Mr. Stone would back down, said that he would just have the building materials loaded back up and take them back to Panama City. Mr. Stone then told the young man that the materials were on his property, therefore; that made them his property.

The young man said that he would just go get the Law and at that time, Mr. Stone told him that he was the Law and that the "Law" maintains that the building materials belong to the property owner.

The smart young man, realizing that he had been backed into a corner, was forced to go back and tell Mr. Martin what he had done and what had happened. He was immediately fired. Mr. Martin then rushed back down to St. Joe to see if he could salvage the original deal. When he asked about the deal, Mr. Stone said, "Sure we still have a deal. I was just trying to teach that young whippersnapper a lesson".

The Port Theatre opened for business the following year on June 20, 1938. The rest is history.

CHAPTER 14

A 3-YEAR OLD KID WINS A WWII BOMB AT THE PORT THEATRE

Most of you from Port St. Joe know that the Port Theatre opened for business in 1938. On one cool Saturday morning in 1944, my sister (Virginia Swatts Harrison) took me to the Saturday morning matinee at the theatre. I was only three (3) years old at the time.

On this particular day, they were having a drawing for a kid's toy. You just had to have a ticket stub to be eligible to win. Before the movie started, the lights were turned on and the Theatre Manager walked up on the stage to facilitate the drawing. When the ticket number was called out, no one said anything. When he announced the number for the second time, my sister asked me where my stub was. I searched my pockets and sure enough, right down in the bottom of my jeans pocket was my stub. My sister quickly checked the number and realized it was the winner. She hollered, "right here" and away we went down front to climb up on that huge stage.

I didn't really understand just what was happening, but I was excited to make my first stage debut. Once the manager checked the ticket number, he declared me to be the winner of a push-toy, made in the shape of a WW II bomb. It had t-stick steering with one wheel on the front and two wheels on the back. It also had a seat. When you sat on the seat, you pushed with your feet (see picture below).

What a ride that was, all over that stage I pushed with the audience clapping. I was having a good time. I forgot all about the show that we came to see and soon had to be ushered back to my seat. I wouldn't let go of that toy though, as it shared the same seat with me throughout the movie. I couldn't wait to get out of that theatre so that I could ride that toy.

I remember riding it until my 5th birthday, when my granddaddy gave me a tri-bike. The tri-bike was a large tricycle with a chain. I lost track of the push-toy after that but as I think back, I think it might have burned up in our garage in about 1946. (That's another story).

About a year ago, I was watching the American Pickers TV show. On this particular show, Mike and Frank were picking a friend's barn somewhere in Kansas. As they started to leave, Mike looked up in the rafters and spotted a bomb looking push-toy. He asked his friend if he could take it down so he could get a better look.

After a few questions about the toy, his friend said that it was one of only two (2) ever made and no one knew what ever happened to the other one. The other one must have been the one that I won at the Port Theatre in 1944, because it looked exactly the same except mine was new. How about that?

CHAPTER 15

OUR FIRST TELEPHONE

In January 1945, we moved from 7th Street to 8th Street when we purchased the A.M. Jones home. I was four years old. When we lived on 7th Street, we did not have a telephone.

Now Mrs. Jones, built the Jones Apartments out on Monument Avenue between 16th and 17th Streets and had moved way out there to live and manage her apartments. Because there were no telephone lines that far out, she was unable to have her telephone moved to that location. This was good for us because we were able to keep the telephone at the 8th Street location. Our telephone number was 104.

There may have been only two Telephone Operators at the time. One of them was Mrs. Alice Williams. Mrs. Williams was married to Mr. Ben Williams and had two boys, both friends of mind, Jimmy and Bo Williams.

Well.... all you had to do was pick up the telephone receiver and the operator would ask, "What number please?" and you would tell her the number you wished to call. My dad had a grocery store downtown and the number was 63J. The "J" indicated that the number was a party-line. When I placed a call to Daddy's store, I would ask Miss Alice to "Please ring my daddy's store." She would reply, "Just one moment, Higdon." Now, just how do think she knew who I was? I realized, when I got older, those Telephone Operators knew everybody and everything.

This is a picture of our first telephone.

CHAPTER 16

BIG FOOT SPOTTED IN GULF COUNTY, FL? LEGEND OR MYTH?

For hundreds of years, there have been many stories told about large hairy hominoids being seen in many parts of the world. The early Native American Kwakliutis Tribe, who were located in the Pacific Northwest, were said to be among the first to report sightings of these large hairy creatures in that area as well as up into Canada. Some were reported to be as tall as 6 to 8 feet. I am not personally aware of any true stories related to such sightings in Gulf County, except......

Sometime after World War II ended, my Uncle Jesse (Stone) returned from serving in the U.S. Navy. One day, when I was about 6 years old, I went for a ride out to Indian Pass with Uncle Jesse. On the way there, we passed by Money Bayou and he told me a story about some Pirates who came ashore there many years ago to hide their stolen treasures. He even showed me a hole where it was said to be the exact location where the treasures were buried. Legend has it that many people have searched the area thoroughly with no treasure ever reported to be found. Could it be that some of the treasures may have been found and just not reported? Maybe....

As we continued our trip, we soon reached Indian Pass where

the road ends. As Uncle Jesse looked across the Pass, he pointed to St. Vincent Island and said that he was reminded of a story that he had heard just before going into the Navy. Seems that in the early 1940's, there were four men from Wewahitchka logging somewhere close to the Apalachicola River near Howard Creek. Three of the four men reportedly spotted a large hairy man, said to have been about 8-feet-tall, running towards the river. The creature moved very fast and was soon out of sight. The fourth man, who was working about 100 feet away, later said that he had not seen what the others had seen. It couldn't have been Big Foot because the name "Big Foot" was not even coined until 1958.

As the story goes, when the four men emerged from the swamp, they discussed what they had seen and decided that they would not mention the sighting to anyone else for fear of alarming women and children living in the area. Most younger men were away fighting in WWII. They decided to devise a plan to capture the creature, remove him from the area and possibly relocate him to St. Vincent Island. That plan was quickly eliminated since one of the men reported that he had just heard that St. Joe Lumber and Export Company had just entered into a contract to harvest timber from the island and was planning to build a temporary bridge across from the island to Indian Pass to transport the timber to the Saw Mill in Port St. Joe.

With no real plan yet settled on, the four men set out to capture the large hairy creature with the idea that maybe they would just turn the wild man over to the authorities and let them decide his fate. It was reported that the men searched for about two more weeks without seeing any other signs of the creature. Apparently, one or more of the men did in fact tell of the sighting, since Uncle Jesse certainly had heard it from someone.

Serious researchers tell of a deep history of sightings of these large hairy men as far back as the arrival of the white man in North America. Much has been written about the myths and so-called legends of Big Foot but so far, no credible evidence has ever become a reality....... that we know about.

CHAPTER 17

SIX (6) NICKELS FOR A QUARTER?

Back in the late 1940's, we used to go to Tallahassee to visit my grandmother several times a year. On Highway 20, about eight (8) miles this side of Tallahassee was an old country store owned by an older gentleman by the name of Owens.

Mr. Owens would sit in a chair outside the store and wave to all the cars going by. Back in those days, he probably didn't get to wave to more than 10 or 20 cars a day.

One day, as we were passing by, Mr. Owens waved to us and Daddy said, "Let's go back to that store and get a Coke." Of course, that was always a treat to us kids, you know, to get a Coke and to stop and visit with Mr. Owens and everything.

Now Cokes were only a nickel in those days and Mr. Owens had one of those newfangled automatic Coke vending machines that took a nickel if you expected to get a Coke out of that machine.

My daddy was always pranking someone, so he asked Mr. Owens if he had six (6) nickels for a quarter? Mr. Owens quipped right back and said, "No Sir, nickels have gone up."

Daddy had been out pranked.

CHAPTER 18

IN TROUBLE TWICE ON MY FIRST DAY OF SCHOOL

On my first day of school, I managed to get myself into trouble not just one time but twice that day. The year was 1947 and I was six (6) years old. We lived on 8th Street in Port St. Joe, so I was able to walk to elementary school which was located on the corner of 9th Street and Long Avenue. The old school sat on the site where the nursing home is now.

The old school was actually a neighborhood school because most of the kids attending lived within a few blocks. I knew the area very well because I played early on with Jimmy and Bo Williams, Kenneth Hurlbut, Bobby Scott, and all of the Kilbourn kids, who all lived very close to the school.

I remember being very excited about going to school on that first day because my older brother and sister had told me so many stories about the fun they had in school. When I got there, a teacher named Minnie Howell (that was Mrs. Howell to us) greeted us and assigned us all a desk. During the first hour or so, Mrs. Howell explained to us what we would be learning while attending first grade. Next, she explained that we would have recess and would be able to go outside to play on the playground equipment. The playground equipment consisted of two sliding boards and some monkey bars. She explained that the larger sliding board was not to be used by us first graders because it was only to be used by the larger boys and girls in the higher grades.

Finally, it was time for recess, and we all ran outside to get on the equipment to play. I noticed that the line to get on the smallest sliding board was pretty long, but no one was using the larger one, so you know where I went from there. I climbed way up to the top of the large slide and positioned myself to have a long smooth ride down. When I got to the bottom, I slid right off into a big mud puddle, bottom side first. I got up and quickly looked around to see if anyone had seen me make my blunder, and then I tore off across the playground towards home. I knew I had to get home and get me a change of pants and underwear RIGHT THEN or all the other kids would be laughing and laughing at me.

When I got home, my mother was not very happy with her first grader. I quickly got my spanking and change of clothes only to be hurried back out the door towards the school. When I reached the school, the Principal, most of the teachers and some of the kids were outside looking for me. Once I was spotted, I was quickly escorted to my classroom and told to stand in the corner for a long, long time (30 minutes).

After my "punishment" was complete, Mrs. Howell told me to return to my desk. On the way to my desk, a little girl named Betty, I think that was her name, grabbed me and kissed me on the cheek and I quickly slapped her. Never did reach my desk because I was told to go back to my corner for an additional 30 minutes. Don't ever remember telling my mother about the "corner thingy".

CHAPTER 19

ELZIE SAVED MY LIFE

Back in the day when I was about 7 or 8 years old, I used to go down to the St. Joe City Pier to play quite often and I loved it.

During the early days, there was an asphalt walkway that started at Hwy 98 in front of Motel St. Joe, (Port Inn today) and went all the way to the beach where it connected to a wooden walkway that extended all the way out to the end of the pier. There was no other access to the pier at that time such as they have today.

At the end of the pier, was a diving board that was used primarily by adults and mostly older kids. Us young kids had a "shallow spot" which was located on the left side of the pier about twenty-five (25) yards from the end. We would jump off the pier in water which was about 4 to 5 feet deep and would climb back up on the pilings to the walkway and do it all over again.

One day some big boys were swimming and diving off of the end of the pier and I decided to go out there and watch. Now there was a big old boy named Tommy who lived at Kenny's Mill and was known to be a bully. Not only was he a bully, he was a mean bully. On that particular day, Tommy picked me up and threw me off the end of the pier. Not being able to swim, I was thrashing around in the water, going under and scared to death. Another big boy was swimming nearby and reached out and pulled me up. He hollered at me, "Boy, can't you swim?" Getting my breath back, I uttered, "No." He said, "Well you are fixing to learn."

It only took a few minutes for him to show me how to dog paddle and just a little while longer for him to teach me how to swim. I just watched what he did and before I knew it, I was swimming good enough to make my way back over to the ladder and climb out of the water and up on the pier.

I will never forget the boy that taught me to swim. He had also told that "bully" to leave me alone and not bother me anymore. He became a friend that I looked up to. His name was Elzie Williams and he still lives in Port St. Joe today. I see him often at McDonalds. I will never forget him. He saved my life.

CHAPTER 20

THE PALL MALL CAPER

When I was about 7 years old, my big brother Ralph was about 10. The Howell's who lived next door had a son named Jimmy Howell. Jimmy was also about 10. Now Jimmy was known to get into trouble pretty often and was always getting caught. It was like Jimmy could just think about doing something wrong and his mother could somehow read it on his face. His mother's name was Callie Howell. That was "Ms. Callie" to my brother and me.

One day Jimmy came over to our house with a sheepish look on his face and said, "Let's go across the street in the woods. I've got something to show you." Now he was talking to my brother but I somehow managed to slip across the street also, being careful so that they would not see me until I was already with them.

It was then and there that Jimmy pulled out of his pocket a whole pack of Pall Mall cigarettes. "Where did you get those?" my brother asked. "Off my mother's kitchen table" replied Jimmy. "Did you bring any matches?" was the next question Ralph uttered. Before he had gotten it out of his mouth good, Jimmy pulled the matches out of his other pocket.

I don't remember much conversation going on during the next 45 minutes while the three of us smoked all twenty of those cigarettes one right after the other. I do remember after we finished, Ralph saying that we smelled like a walking cigarette and that we were going to get into big trouble when our mothers smelled it on us. Jimmy was smarter than us, I remember thinking, because he blurted out, "All we got to do is chew up some green pine straw and

42

they won't smell nothing." Well we did just that and we no longer smelled (so we thought) like cigarettes. We then decided that it was time to go on home.

That night Ralph and I both got sick on our stomachs and threw up half the night. My mother was busy trying to take care of us and of course she began to wonder how come we both got sick at the same time. When she questioned us, Ralph told her it must have been something we ate. Mother then went into the kitchen and threw out all of the leftovers, thinking that Ralph must have been right.

The next day, we went next door to see Jimmy. Ms. Callie invited us in and said that Jimmy was in the bed and that we could go on in to see him. Ralph and I went to his room and there was Jimmy laying there with his eyes all red and a look on his face that I had never witnessed. We asked if he had gotten sick the night before and he said, "No, but just look at my Butt." He pulled the sheet back and there was the blackish-bluish butt that I had ever seen. Ralph asked, "What the devil happen to you?" Jimmy spoke up saying, "I told the Truth."

Now....I figure the lesson you learn from all this is, you don't mess with Ms. Callie's Pall Malls.

CHAPTER 21

A WOULD-BE GARAGE & A TREE

After World War II ended, my uncle, Mickey (Stone), returned to the University of Florida to finish law school. In about 1948, he returned to Port St. Joe and established a law office. The next year, he purchased a new 1949 Dodge. Now Uncle Mickey, being a single man at the time, lived with his parents (my grandparents, Mr. and Mrs. T.H. "Higdon" Stone). One day he asked my Granddaddy for permission to build a garage next to Granddaddy's house. Granddaddy told him that it would be ok and soon after that, construction of the garage began.

Just prior to the garage being finished, Granddaddy noticed that the garage doors were being installed facing Highway 98 and not the alley in the rear. That day when Uncle Mickey came home, Granddaddy asked him how he was going to get his car in the garage since there was a small tree growing in front of the garage doors. Uncle Mickey replied, "That's simple Daddy, I'm planning on cutting the tree down." Granddaddy spoke up and said, "Now wait a minute Son. You asked me for permission to build a garage. You didn't say anything about cutting my tree down". From the day of completion, that garage never had a car parked in it until.... fast forward your thinking to the year 1962 for the rest of this two-part story.

In 1962, I purchased a 1960 Austin Healey. Knowing that I was soon going to National Guard Training, I began to think about where I would store the Healey while I was gone. It occurred to me that I might be able to get that small car in Uncle Mickey's garage if I inched it in around that tree which by now had grown into a rather large tree. The first step was to measure the width of the car and also the width between the tree and the garage doors. Once I was convinced that the car would clear the tree, I went inside the garage and moved all the junk over to one side, making room for the car. Then, it was just a matter of carefully driving the car around that tree. Once inside, I reversed the process and with much care, I managed to back it out without hitting the tree.

Now, I just needed to get permission from Uncle Mickey to use the garage, since my granddaddy had passed away in 1958. I hurried down to Uncle Mickey's Office to ask. He was walking out of his office just as I parked directly in front. I quickly got out and said, "Uncle Mickey, I was wondering if you would mind if I store my car in your garage while I go to National Guard Training?" He quipped right back at me and said, "Hell no, Daddy wouldn't let me cut that tree down and you sure as hell ain't gonna cut it down either." I quickly replied as I pointed to the little car, "Oh, no Sir, I have already inched my car around the tree into the garage and it was no problem." He then fired back, as he looked down at my car, "Well ok, as long as you don't cut that tree down."

That garage stood for many years with me having the knowledge that I had owned the only car that had ever been parked in it. There has always been a story around town, that there had never been a car in that garage because of Granddaddy's tree. Not true.... because I was the one who made it happen.

CHAPTER 22

ODD JOBS I HAD GROWING UP IN PORT ST. JOE

Watching kids today wasting their time using their cell phones and other social media tools reminds me of some of the odd jobs I had when growing up. I remember when I was about eight (8) years old, I was too young to mow grass other than our front yard. I was unable to push the old rotary lawn mower through the grass if it got as high as six inches tall. I was always trying to figure some way to earn a little spending money. My folks didn't just give us money to spend. We had to earn our own.

I had just had a birthday and my mother and daddy had given me a wagon as my main gift. I usually got school clothes since my July birthday was so close to the starting date of school each year. Of course, I wasn't allowed to wear the new clothes until the first day of school. The wagon was a nice birthday present but none of the kids in the neighborhood wanted to pull me up and down the street in my wagon. Most of them were older than me and had other interests, so I put my mind to working, trying to figure out how I was going to make some money with that wagon. It seemed like nothing would come to mind.

One day I went with Daddy down to the Sinclair Station to buy gas. Daddy would always buy us a coke or in my case a nu-grape soda when we went with him. Mr. Morgan Jones, who owned the station reminded us to be sure to return the drink bottles to receive a deposit refund. Back in those days, bottles were returned to the bottling plant and reused. Stores would pay you 2 cents per bottle when you returned them. Now most people would not bother and would just throw the bottles away. It was then and there that I figured out just how I was going to make use of my wagon and make me some money.

As we left the station, we stopped next door at Cheech's Laundry and Dry Cleaning to pick up a dress of my mother's that had been left there to be cleaned. While we were waiting, a lady brought in 100 clothes hangers and was paid a half cent for each one she returned. Wow! That was 50 cents just like that. Now my mind began to go into overtime. I knew where I could get plenty of bottles and plenty of clothes hangers. The next day I got busy with my wagon and started collecting. Bottles were easy to find and not only that, people would give them to you, so they didn't have to fool with returning them themselves. It was the same with clothes hangers too. By midafternoon, I had returned enough bottles and clothes hangers to make plenty of spending money.

As I got a little older, I had a couple of paper routes and while in high school, worked in a grocery store and in a men's store. I also planted pine trees one year for St. Joseph Land & Development Company during Christmas break. It was not hard to find a job. You just had to ask and be willing to work.

I'm thinking kids today would be better off if they would get out and earn their own money. Maybe they would learn the importance of saving and becoming responsible adults. Not much humor in this story, just reminiscing about how it was for kids as we grew up in Port St. Joe.

CHAPTER 23

A LESSON TO BE LEARNED ABOUT PAYING YOUR BILLS

When I was about ten (10) years old, I belonged to the Cub Scouts in Port St. Joe. Now my mother, just one (1) month before, bought me a new pair of Cub Scout shoes and in that period of time I had managed to scuff them up to the point you could not recognize the fact that they were supposed to be part of the Cub Scout uniform. I mean the soles had even come loose and were turned back towards the heels making it hard to even walk. Some of you who were rough on shoes as a boy know what I mean.

Not wanting my mother to see how bad I had ruined my shoes, I went downtown to Austin-Atchison Men's Store to look at new shoes. Austin-Atchison's was next door to what is now the Great Wall Restaurant located at 412 Reid Avenue. The Store Manager at the time was Marion Parker. As I walked around the store looking at everything, I managed to finally look at a new pair of Cub Scout shoes. Marion (Mr. Parker to me) asked me if I liked those shoes and I told him that I did. He then said, "Why don't you buy them?" I told him I didn't have any money. Mr. Parker replied, "You have a paper route, don't you?" I said "Yes Sir." and he then said "You can charge them and pay $2.00 per week." Not ever having charged anything in my life, I said "You'd let me charge these shoes?" He then explained what it meant to charge and pay on the debt until it was paid off. I was so proud to be making the "first charge" of my life.

I began to think that maybe I could hide the old shoes so that my mother wouldn't know and of course, I would have to scuff up the new shoes a bit because she would surely know something was up if she saw that I had new ones. This seemed like a good plan at the time and sure enough I pulled it off without her knowing what I had done.

Just as I planned, each week I would go in the store and pay $2.00 on my "account". Sometime after about a month, I was unable to pay my weekly payment because some of my customers failed to pay me for their paper and maybe also because I had been drinking too many 25 cent milk shakes at Buzzett's Drug Store next door. Anyway, I didn't have enough money to pay my debt. Two or three days later I saw Mr. Parker walking down Reid Avenue and to keep him from seeing me, I crossed the street. I didn't like the feeling I had, knowing that I owed that debt and having to hide from Mr. Parker, so I went home and told my mother what I had done and about it bothering me. My mother wasn't very happy but gave me the money to pay off the debt, making sure that I knew that I would now be paying her back. I think she realized that I had learned a valuable lesson. Since that time, I have been very careful about what I bought and always made sure I could pay back any debt I made. I will always believe that this lesson was one of the best I ever learned.

CHAPTER 24

THE LORD AND THE DEVIL DIVIDING UP SOULS

I used to ride my bike all over Port St. Joe and late one afternoon, I rode to Oak Grove and on out the Niles Road to Holly Hill Cemetery. I must have been about twelve (12) years old at the time. Ward Ridge had never even been thought of, at that time.

There used to be a big old pecan tree just inside the cemetery fence. I didn't know it at the time, but there were two boys, out of sight, who had filled up a bucket of pecans and began dividing them between themselves. "One for you, one for me, one for you, one for me", said one of the boys. A couple of pecans fell out of the bucket and rolled down by the fence.

As I came riding down the road on my bicycle, I thought I heard voices from inside the cemetery and I slowed down to investigate. Sure enough, I heard, "One for you, one for me, one for you, one for me..." It was then and there that I realized what it was, and I jumped back on my bicycle and started back toward Oak Grove. Just as I was approaching the railroad tracks, I spotted an old man, walking with a cane alongside of the tracks. "Come here quick." I hollered, "You won't believe what I just heard! Satan and the Lord are out at the cemetery dividing up souls!" The old man said, "Beat it boy, I ain't got no time for no foolish tales." After I insisted that he go with me back to the cemetery, he finally agreed and hobbled slowly down the road to the cemetery. Standing next to the fence and carefully staying out of site, we heard "One for you, one for me, one for you, one for me." The old man whispered to me, "Boy, you was a telling me da truth. Let's see if we can see the Lord".... Being afraid, we peered through the fence, yet were still unable to see anything. The old man and I gripped the wrought iron bars of the fence tighter and tighter as we tried to get a glimpse of the Lord. Then we heard, "One for you, one for me. That's all. Now let's go get those two nuts by the fence and we'll be done."

Now the old man had the lead for a good quarter-mile back towards the tracks before I ran over his cane and passed him on my bike. It was one of the few times that I made it home before dark. I never told this story to anybody because who'd ever believed that the old man coulda outrun me on my bicycle.

CHAPTER 25

WAS THE PTA MEETING THE MAIN EVENT?

When I was about twelve years old, I used to get on my bike and ride all over Port St. Joe, visiting with friends, exploring roads that I had never been down and stopping to play with playmates on the school playground. I knew it was my business to be home before dark or I had a different kind of "business" to deal with.

Port St. Joe Elementary School was only about two blocks from where I lived and every month they had a PTA (Parent-Teachers Association) meeting at the school house auditorium. On one occasion, my sister drove my mother to the school house to attend the PTA meeting.

Now.... my mother felt like it was her job to attend the meeting, being that she was the President of the association and everything. My sister had driven her to the meeting in her 1950 Plymouth and parked it right in front of the middle building, parallel to the sidewalk, taking up at least two parking spaces. On this particular night, my daddy happened to be working and I was told that I could either go to the PTA meeting or stay at home. I decided to just stay home at least until my mother and sister were out of sight.

Once I couldn't see the tail lights of that old Plymouth, I got on my bike and headed on over to the Elementary School. Being that it was past time for the meeting to start, I noticed that they must have had a good turn out because of the number of cars parked on Long Avenue in front of the school. I jumped off my bike and hid it behind a palm tree, making my way over to my sister's car.

Sure as shooting, the keys to the car were right where I knew they would be, under the floor mat. I climbed in that old Plymouth, quickly started 'er up and looked around to see if anybody had seen me. With nobody looking, I backed that car out into Long Avenue and proceeded to make my way down toward Eleventh Street where I would make a U-turn. After turning around, I slowly drove that old car back up Long Avenue and just about the time I got even with the parking space I had just exited, I looked over and saw that another car seemed to have gotten my parking place.

It scared me so much because I knew my mother and sister would know that the car had been moved. While looking at the other car, I veered off the road to the right and the right front corner of the old Plymouth bumper made a glancing blow with the left rear bumper of Bud Taylor's daddy's 1949 Packard which was parked in front of the water tower. My guess was that Mr. and Mrs. Taylor were also attending that PTA meeting.

Well....about that time my racing heart jumped clear out of my chest and sailed through the open window of the car and was making a flapping sound on the pavement. I somehow managed to stop the car, get out, retrieve my heart and begin to access the damage. Lucky for me, there was nary a scratch on either bumper. Man, those old cars could take a licking and keep on clicking or something like that.

It was then and there that I decided that this joy-ride was fixing to be over real quick. I got back in the car and proceeded on down to Ninth Street, made another U-turn and headed back down the street to hopefully find a parking place close to where I started from.

As luck would have it, the car that I thought had gotten my place had left enough room for me to squeeze the old Plymouth in at an angle instead of parallel to the sidewalk. I quickly put the keys back under the mat and piled out of that car. Within seconds, I was on my bike hightailing it back home.

When mother and sister got home, nothing was said about the car being moved and so I assumed that they had not noticed. It would be a long time before I would be brave enough to "borrow" any of our cars again. In fact, I don't believe that I ever did. Now....my bother Ralph? That's another story.

CHAPTER 26

FIRST CORVETTE IN PORT ST. JOE

In 1953, this was the first Corvette ever sold in Port St. Joe. It was sold by Garraway Chevrolet Company which was located on Williams Avenue. At the age of 12, I first saw this car in the dealers show room and thought it was the most beautiful automobile I had ever seen. It was purchased by Mr. Arbogast, who drove it to work at St. Joe Paper Company because it was made of fiberglass and it would not rust. Since 1953 was the first year for the Corvette, it would be interesting to know what the Vin number was.

I remember at some point and time, I believe in the late 60's, Mr. Arbogast purchased all new chrome for the car since that was the only thing to rust on the car. Mr. Arbagast also owned a 1958 Pontiac Bonneville which is also a collectable automobile. In about 1970, he traded both the Corvette and the Bonneville to my brother at Swatts Motor Company for a 1965 Cadillac which had been owned by Dick McIntosh and his wife Big Sara.

Shortly after that, my brother sold the Corvette to Binky Kilbourn. After about a year, Binky sold it to a man from somewhere in Alabama. Someone in Parker, Florida bought the Bonneville and kept it for quite some time. It was sold again just a few years ago to a friend of mine here in Panama City. It remains in his care to this day.

CHAPTER 27

FAMILY IN TROUBLE

There's a story about one of the times in the 1950's, when my brother stole Daddy's Hudson, if anyone is interested.

My dad would go out on the freight train every other night and leave his Hudson parked and locked up in front of the AN Railroad Depot. My brother Ralph, who knew where the spare keys were hidden, would often take the keys and go down to the Depot to steal the Hudson. He would unlock the car, get in and undo the speedometer cable, then check to see how much gas it had so he could be sure to replace it when the joy-ride was over. He would then go pick up his joy-ride buddies.

On this particular occasion, he picked up Binky Kilbourn, Jackie Davis, Dan Hatfield and Jimmy Howell. Once they were all on board, off to Blountstown they went for their joy-ride. On the turn-a-round trip back to Port St. Joe, they came through Wewa, running a little slightly over the speed limit. Up ahead, one of the boys hollered, "There's Hersey."

Now, Hersey was the only Gulf County Sheriff's Deputy at that time and he was known to hang around Wewa a lot, being that Wewa was the County Seat and housed the Jailhouse and.....everythang. When Ralph saw that it was indeed Deputy Hersey, he started blinking the headlights off and on and blowing the horn. The old Hudson breezed through Wewa doing about 50 MPH as if there was an emergency. When Deputy Hersey spotted them and of course not having any kind of radio communications in those days, rushed back to the jail to use the telephone to call the Port St. Joe Police

Department to report a "family in trouble", must be headed to the hospital and to please assist in any way possible to assure that they made it without incident.

A few minutes later, when the old Hudson rolled into Port St. Joe on Hwy 71, the boys could see the police car up ahead at Hwy 98 and there was Patrolman Kelly, with the red light flashing on his patrol car, blocking Hwy 98 traffic, so that the "family in trouble" could make their way on to the hospital. Patrolman Kelly was standing out in the middle of Hwy 98, flagging the old Hudson on through the turn. As soon as he finished assisting them, Patrolman Kelly got into his patrol car and headed for the hospital in order to see what the emergency was all about.

Now the boys knew that he would find out shortly that there was no emergency and would soon start looking for the old Hudson. That's when they realized that they might better travel on to Apalachicola and not return until after dark. It was wintertime and dark came early, so the old Hudson crept back into town and slowly took the boys home one by one. Jimmy Howell was worried about getting his tail beat for being gone all afternoon and the others were worried that Officer Kelly might spot them on the way home. Dan Hatfield, who often stuttered when he got excited, had been begging to go home for about two hours. As soon as they were all home, Ralph rushed back down to the Depot to return the Hudson. The boys never got caught and Daddy never found out. They were all lucky.

CHAPTER 28

MR. GUERTIN'S NEW OLDSMOBILE HOLIDAY 98 COUPE

One day in 1955, Carlos Guertin of Port St. Joe, got off work from the Paper Mill and got into his old rusty Studebaker pickup truck and headed to Panama City to buy a new car. Now Carlos was a well thought of older gentleman who was probably one of the highest hourly paid employees who worked at the mill.

On this particular day, being dressed in his dirty work clothes, he headed to the Panama City Cadillac Dealership which was located downtown on Harrison Avenue. Arriving in the old truck, he got out and went inside the showroom to look at the new Cadillacs. Now there were several salesmen standing around and some of them were probably making comments about the poor dirty looking old man over there who probably couldn't even buy a gallon of gas, much less, a new Cadillac. And so, when no one came over to help him, he decided it was time to go.

Carlos had remembered that there was an Oldsmobile Dealership over on 4th Street and he proceeded to drive over there. The name of the dealer was Harrison Oldsmobile. Once he arrived, he went inside to the showroom, and walked over to look at a beautiful 1955 Oldsmobile 98 Holiday Coupe. Very soon, he was greeted by a very friendly salesman, who asked how he could help. Carlos looked at the sticker price on the window and asked, "Is this the price of this car?" The salesman replied, "Yes sir." Carlos then told him "Fine, I want to buy it." They then went into the office and the salesmen asked Carlos did he want to finance the car. Carlos pulled out a bag of cash and said, "no I want to pay for it."

It is not known if the salesmen at the Cadillac Dealership ever knew what had happened, but if they did, I'm sure their attitude towards people in work clothes, probably changed for the better.

CHAPTER 29

TELEPHONE COMPANY LOGO & EDWARD BALL

In about 1955, St. Joseph Telephone & Telegraph Company installed the first dial system within it's company exchanges. It was customary for telephone companies back then to assign both an alphabetical and numerical prefix to each new telephone number. All telephone numbers had to be changed to a 7-digit number in order for the new dial system to work.

In the Port St. Joe exchange, BA7 and BA9 were assigned for the 227 and 229 exchange prefixes. Example: 227-5555 & 229-6555. The BA on your telephone dial represented 22, so if you were dialing BA7-5555, you would actually dial 227-5555. The BA was derived from the first two letter of the name Ball. For those of you that never heard of him, Edward Ball was the Chairman of St. Joe Paper Company and since the telephone company was owned by the Paper Company, Mr. Ball also carried the title of President of St. Joseph Telephone & Telegraph Company until about 1971.

Each of the telephone company's 13 exchanges such as Apalachicola, Wewahitchka, Blountstown etc. all had their own alphabetical and numerical prefixes relating to a name. At the moment, I would be hard pressed to remember all of the related names for the prefixes in all of the other exchanges, but I think maybe you get the picture of what I am trying to say.

At some point and time, all of the alphabetical designations were dropped but the numerical prefixes remained the same, therefore; no number changes were necessary when this was done. For example, the number BA7-5555 actually became 227-5555.

The logo chosen at the time that the dial system was installed, had the name of the company with an image of a telephone in the center. Behind the telephone was a ball, designed to look like a baseball, which just happened to be the last name of Edward Ball. See the image of the old logo below.

CHAPTER 30

TWO YOUNG BOYS, TWO CARS & A DUSTY ROAD

In 1955, when I was 14 years old, the Florida Department of Transportation began building a new highway from Port St. Joe to Apalachicola. The old highway, which still exist today, followed the coast through the Indian Pass area and on to Apalachicola. The new road, paralleling the railroad tracks, would cut off several miles between the two towns.

One Sunday afternoon, I was riding around St. Joe in my car and stopped to talk to Glenn Alligood. Glenn was driving his daddy's 1951 Pontiac. Glenn suggested that we ride out to check on the progress of the new Depot Creek Bridge, which was about 8 miles out of St. Joe on the new highway. I told Glenn to go ahead and I would follow him out to the bridge. I don't know why we didn't go in one car, but I suspect it was probably because we both wanted to drive our own cars.

Now the new road was being prepared for paving but had not yet been paved. The road bed was mostly shell and dirt. It was packed pretty well but was mighty dusty. As Glenn proceeded on the dirt road, he must have been traveling about 40 to 50 mph and I was right behind him. That old Pontiac was throwing up so much dust that most of the time, I couldn't even see it. After a few minutes, all of a sudden, I thought I saw brake lights up ahead. Sure enough, that old Pontiac was braking. I panicked and slammed on my brakes and began to slide, first to the left and then to the right and then left again. I thought sure I was going to hit

64

Glenn's car, but ended up straddling a big old pile of dirt on the side of the road.

I was shaking so bad that my brain and the rest of my body was out of sync. In other words, I couldn't function for a few moments. I was finally able to put the car in reverse and back off the pile of dirt. Now Glenn had seen the whole thing in his rear-view mirror and had just about driven into the creek to keep me from hitting him. He soon exited his car and came back to see if I was ok. I assured him that I was and we both agreed that we might ought to turn around and get ourselves back to Port St. Joe. It was a slow drive back to town. Neither of us told anyone else about what happened for obvious reasons. After 62 years, I guess it's safe enough to tell about it now.

CHAPTER 31

JUST CHARGE IT TO DADDY

Back in the late 1950's while attending Port St. Joe High
School, many of my friends and I would go downtown after school
to Smith's Pharmacy for an after-school snack. At that time,
Smith's still had a soda fountain and in addition to sodas, you could
get ice cream, milk shakes, malts, banana splits, sandwiches and
much more. For those of you that don't remember Smith's
Pharmacy, it was located on the corner of Reid Avenue and Third
Street, in the same building as the present Sister's Restaurant. John
Robert Smith was the owner and operator (Pharmacist).

Most of the time, because I worked, I had money to purchase
my favorite snacks, which was a spiced ham sandwich and a milk
shake. At times, it might be a banana split. During one period of
time, I was in between after school jobs and wasn't as flush as I
normally would have been. This was a period of about one month,
that funds were, let's just say, not readily available but that didn't
deter my appetite and my desires for my snacks. It was during this
time that my backup plan was put into place. When Mrs. Sue
Roberts would come to take our orders, I would just order my
usual. During that month, having no money to pay with, I would
just merely tell Mrs. Roberts to charge it to my Daddy. On
occasion, Mrs. Roberts would raise her eyebrows at me, but would
jot it down and add it to the other charges I had made during that
month.

My plan to charge my snacks had worked very well that
month, until the bills were mailed out the first of the next month.
It was then and there that my Daddy made me aware of what the

word reality really meant. Without going into any detail, let's just say that my desires to "Just charge it to Daddy" were forever erased from my vocabulary.

CHAPTER 32

MAX MADE HIS MARK

In one of my previous stories, I made mention of the fact that in 1912, Mr. & Mrs. A.M. Jones had built the house that I grew up in. One of their sons, A. Morgan Jones Jr. used to own and run the Sinclair Service Station in Port St. Joe back in the 1950's. It was located on the corner of 4th Street and Monument Avenue next to Creech's Laundry.

When I was about 16, I stopped in at the station one day and visited with Mr. Morgan (Jones) as I often did. Mr. Morgan told me a story about something his older brother Max had done when growing up in our old house. It seems that one day Max was bored, so he decided to print his name on the back wall of his bedroom with his 22-caliber single action riffle. Max fired several shots with that single-shot 22 caliber rifle into the back wall and managed to print the letters MA, before his mother reached the bedroom and stopped him. To print those two letters with small holes meant a lot of locking and loading and firing of that riffle.

After hearing this story, I went home to see if I could still see the holes made by Max with that small 22 cal. riffle and sure enough I could see them right up close to the ceiling of that back wall just as Mr. Morgan had said. The wall had probably been repainted several times over the years, but you could still see the small holes in the wall, which spelled MA.

Jimmy and Cheryl Johnson's daughter, Julie, owns the house now and one day, a few years ago, as she was showing me the house and the improvements that she had made, I pointed out the holes to her that Max had made on that back wall and of course, passed down the story of Max and the 22-caliber rifle. Max had made his mark.

Some of us go through life without ever making our mark.

CHAPTER 33

SMOKE CIGARETTES OR BUY GASOLINE?

When I was 16 years old, I used to ride to school with my friend Larry Henley in his mother's new 1957 Oldsmobile. Each day, Larry would pick me up and head straight down to Frank Pate's Shell Station to buy cigarettes. (Now for those of you who don't know, Frank Pate's Shell Station was located in Port St. Joe, Florida on the corner of Third Street and Highway 98). I always waited in the car while Larry went inside and put 30 cents into a cigarette vending machine for one measly pack of nasty cigarettes.

One day while waiting, I just happened to think about how much money Larry spent in a 30-day month on cigarettes. I suddenly realized that he was spending around $9.00 per month on those awful things. Now that might not seem like much money these days but in 1957, that amounted to a lot of dough. I remember that I compared the cost of the cigarettes to the cost of gasoline, which at that time was about 25 cents a gallon. My calculations astounded me when I realized that the cost of those light'em up if you have'em sticks was equal to the cost of two and a half tanks of gasoline.

Now in 1957, we didn't even know that cigarettes caused cancer, but I remember thinking that I didn't want to waste my money buying those stinking cigarettes, when I could buy enough gasoline to ride many a mile for the same amount of money. That my friends was a pure economic decision that quickly became a no brainer.

In 1957, the average cost of a home was about $10,000.00. The average cost of a car was about $1,800.00 and the average annual income was about $4,500.00.

I did a little checking and the average cost of a pack of cigarettes today in Florida, is $6.29. That's about $189.00 per month for one pack a day. Some people smoke as many as two (2) to three (3) packs a day. You do the math. Now if that doesn't scare you, think about CANCER. I just did the math myself and even at the cost of gasoline today, we can still ride many a mile for what it cost to buy cigarettes.

Now you just heard (read) the "rest of the story".

CHAPTER 34

IF ELVIS PRESLEY HAD GROWN UP IN PORT ST. JOE

If Elvis Presley had grown up in Port St. Joe, this is the 1957 Cadillac Eldorado Convertible that he would have been driving up and down Reid Avenue. He would probably have given St. Joe High School girls rides between the STAC House and the old high school gym. Those who didn't get to ride, would be waving to those who did. High school boys might not have understood what was happening as many of the girls might have even broken up with their "steady's".

Elvis might have even sung a few songs at the STAC House and because of the crowd, he may have had to move the show to the Centennial Building. The City Commission would have probably waived the fee charged for most events being held there because they would be proud to be a part of such a production.

On these occasions, the High School Principal may have even announced that there would be "no home room check" so that the kids could get out of school early enough to get good seating for the show.

Of course, Elvis didn't grow up in Port St. Joe, his parents didn't even live here but, if he had, Graceland might have been built on 50 acres of prime real estate provided at a reasonable price per acre by St. Joe Paper Co.

Just saying............

CHAPTER 35

"BUCK" BIRD EXITS '49 FORD THE HARD WAY

In the mid to late 1950's a bunch of us Port St. Joe High School boys always had something going on, especially on the weekends. Some of us had part-time after school jobs at Mr. Wood's IGA Grocery Store, which was located next to Frank Pate's Service Station on highway 98.

There used to be a Coast Guard Station out on Cape San Blas and some of the young guys in the Coast Guard would come in to the IGA to buy groceries for those assigned to the CG Station. Of course, they always bought the best of everything including the best cut of steaks and most anything else they wanted to eat. Some of us became good friends with them and they would invite us out to the Station to visit and eat with them. They really knew how to prepare those steaks. Most of us had never even had a choice steak. Families back then just couldn't afford to feed several kids steak. Chicken and fish was what most of us were used to and were mighty grateful to get that. Most families had their own chickens and our dads would either catch mullet or buy them for 10 cents a pound down at Simmons Bayou.

Jimmy Fuller's mother bought him a 1949 Ford four door sedan and one Friday night several of us loaded up in that old Ford and went to the Coast Guard Station to eat supper with our Coast Guard buddies. As I remember, there was Jimmy, Alex Gaillard, Frank Fletcher, Buddy "Buck" Bird and myself. Seems to me there must have been a bottle of "sprits" that was passed around to some of the others (not me of course) and on the way back from the Cape somehow that bottle emptied itself. Once back in St. Joe, there seemed to be nothing goin on, so we decided to ride out to the beach to see who was at the "Patio". Not much going on there either, so we road on down to the west end of Mexico Beach to turn around. On the way back to town, when we were going around Dixie Belle Curve, someone discovered that old "Buck" was no longer in the back seat.

Of course, that kinda got our attention and Jimmy quickly turned the old Ford around again and we headed back to the beach to see if we could find Buck. Since we had not stopped anywhere, we figured that the back door had come open when we turned around at Mexico Beach and that Buck must have fallen out then. Soon we reached the beach and low and behold there was Buck trying to thumb a ride back to town.

Now Buck didn't seem to be hurt much but he did have a few scrapes on his arms and his clothes were full of sand spurs. It seems to me that Buck may have uttered a few choice words to us, something about us leaving him for the buzzards or something like that. It was just another Friday night, out with a few buddies in Port St. Joe. Nothing bad but just boys being boys.

CHAPTER 36

OLD YALLOW

My granddaddy once told me that when he was a young man, he had a girlfriend that was so cross-eyed that when she cried, the tears ran down her back. I had never heard anything like this said before, so I asked my mother about it. She said that he shouldn't have told me such a thing and explained to me that I was never to make fun of anyone and that it was wrong. I never forgot what he told me, nor did I forget what my mother said either.

I must tell you that it is hard to tell this story without it appearing that I am making fun of Mrs. Howard, one of my high school math teachers. Now Mrs. Howard was one of my favorite teachers and I loved her for her teaching abilities as well as being such a good sport about all the things we kids came up with. It was a fact though, that she did have an eye impairment of such that when she was looking at you, it appeared that she was looking in the opposite direction.

One day when I happened to be in rare form and sitting in the back of the classroom, I said out loud, "Mrs. Howard?" Appearing to be looking at someone else, she said, "What?" I, of course thought she was looking at someone else, so I repeated myself by saying again, "MRS. HOWARD!" It was then and there that she said, "What do you want, Higdon?" I then replied to her, "Have you seen Ole Yallow?" Not knowing exactly what I was talking about, she said "What are you talking about?" I repeated the question, "Have you seen Ole Yallow?" Mrs. Howard, about this time was getting a little irritated with me and said, "WHAT DO YOU MEAN, OLE YALLOW?" I said, "You know, my ole yallow pencil." Now....with the classmates laughing and the look on her face being less than pleasant, I began to wonder if I would, once again, be headed to Mr. Bowdoin's office for another one of those "conversations" we frequently had. Luck would have it though, when I began my assessment of her reaction, I found that she was laughing just as hard as the rest of us, however; it had been a little hard to tell for sure, since she appeared to be looking in the opposite direction.

I thought it was my job to start the class off each day on a light note. This day, I apparently had accomplished just that.

CHAPTER 37

IF THE HALLS OF OLD PORT ST. JOE HIGH SCHOOL COULD TALK ...

One might hear them say...."Remember that Higdon Swatts always getting into trouble in the halls between classes?" He was either hanging onto the bell to keep it from ringing or acting like "Ruff Rolph".

Now "Ruff Rolph" might have been him or one of his friends running spasticly up behind one of the teachers and stop the foolishment just before the teacher would turn around to see why the other kids were laughing. The "Ruff Rolphs" of St. Joe High sometimes did not stop in time and thus they would be caught and marched down to the Principal's office.

There was one occasion when that Hig Swatts ran up behind Mr. Nicholson, tried to stop but couldn't and slid into one of Mr. Nicholson's heels. Hig, knowing that he had been caught, just lay there on that old dark brown tile floor as if he had fainted. With his eyes being closed in order to fake the faint, he heard someone holler "Get back." When he opened his eyes, he saw Coach Faison leaning over him to see if he was ok. Coach soon realized there was a fake faint going on here and immediately said, "Get up boy and follow me." At this point and time, one did not have to imagine where he would be following the coach.

Once ole Hig reached the Principal's Office, Coach Faison said, "Mr. Bowdoin, I just want to show you what this boy was doing in the hall on his way to class." With that, Coach twisted his body sideways and just fell out (as if to faint) on ole Hig. Now Coach musta weighed about 225 lbs. and Ole Hig about 128 lbs. soakin wet.

Just before both of them hit the floor, Mr. Bowdoin started to laugh. He then said, "Hig, get yo-self back to class and don't be showing up down here at my office no more." (He probably said "yourself" and "anymore", but you know this is them halls a talking and you know them halls ain't never been taught proper English).

The Story ends here with both Mr. Bowdoin and Coach Faison being heard a laughing all the way down to Hig's classroom. Many more stories could be told by them there halls.

CHAPTER 38

PETE COMFORTER AND THE TWO BY FOURS (2X4'S)

Mr. Pete Comforter was Rocky Comforter's dad and back in the day, he owned Comforter's Funeral Home.

One day, back in 1959, Mr. Pete and one of his employees went down to St. Joe Hardware to order some lumber (2x4's). When they got to the store, Pete told his employee to go in and order the lumber from Mr. Ashley Costin. Mr. Pete told him he would just sit and wait for him in the car.

Well the employee did just what Mr. Pete told him to do, but Mr. Ashley then asked him how long he wanted the 2x4's. The employee said, "I'm not sure, let me go back out to the car and ask Mr. Pete." Shortly, the employee re-entered the store and said to Mr. Ashley, "Mr. Pete said we gonna need them for a long time, cause he's gonna build a shed for one of them big old Cadillac Hearse's."

CHAPTER 39

HIGH SCHOOL GRADUATION? "I DOESN'T KNOW"

Back in 1960 when I was a senior at Port St. Joe High School, there was a professional comedian named Dave Gardner, who had made a talk recording entitled "Rejoice Dear Hearts". On his record, Brother Dave, as he liked to call himself, would respond to questions often by saying, "I doesn't know." Now being high school kids, some of us began to repeat this saying almost every time we were asked a question. Most kids thought it was a funny saying but our English teacher, Mrs. Stone was not at all amused and attempted to correct us when she heard us use this "saying".

Toward the end of the year, I was called on to give an oral book report on a certain book that I had been assigned to read. I remember standing, as we were required to do, and telling Mrs. Stone that I could not give the report. She asked why, and I responded, "because I have not read the book." She then asked why I had not read the book and my answer was "I doesn't know." Mrs. Stone, not happy with this response, said she would give me two days to read the book and to make the report or she would not let me graduate.

This was getting serious because I had already spent 13 years toward the goal of finishing high school and I didn't want to spend one more year trying to graduate. For some reason, I never did make that book report, but Mrs. Stone allowed me to go to graduation practice just as if I was going to graduate.

Finally, the big night arrived, and we were all seated on the football field with the Port St. Joe High School "Band of Gold" seated adjacent. As the ceremony began, many speeches were given, and awards were handed out. The next big thing to happen was to be the awarding of diplomas. (We did not know at the time, but when the diplomas were being transported from the school out to the football field, Mrs. Biggs and Ms. Niblack had stumbled and about half of the diplomas had fallen to the ground and had to be placed back into alphabetical order.)

Now fast forward to the main event. Mr. Tommy Owens, who was the Superintendent of Schools was presented the Port St. Joe High School Graduating Class of 1960 for the purpose of awarding the High school diplomas to the members of the class. It was a very exciting time for us graduates and went along very nicely, with the names being called alphabetically right on up until I was next in line.

My name was not called and five other classmates behind me had to step around me in order to receive their diploma. It was during this time that I began to think about what Mrs. Stone had told me about not letting me graduate. It also didn't help that members of the band were whispering out loud that Ole Hig ain't gonna graduate. I'm sure that most other people in the stands were thinking the same thing.

About that time, the Superintendent called my name. It was with great relief and a short "whew" that caused me to advance very quickly up to the podium to receive my reward. Once I was up there, Mr. Owens stepped away from the microphone to ask me who the girl was behind me. I'm sure he did not want to call any more names out of line.

It was then and there that I answered right into the microphone, "I doesn't know." I was so excited to be graduating, I didn't even know what I had said. Of course, the crowd roared with laughter and I later found out that Mrs. Stone had gone into shock.

Afterwards, she told me that she ought to take back that diploma. Good thing for me she was only kidding. All is well today. I am 77 now and can still remember this story as if it were yesterday.

CHAPTER 40

KIDS GROWING UP IN PORT ST. JOE, FL - PART ONE

This is Part One (1) of a three-part story about kids growing up in Port St. Joe, Florida in the 1940's, 1950's and 1960's.

Growing up in Port St. Joe had a lot to offer to kids growing up, contrary to what many people may think. Most small towns the size of St. Joe have very few activities that keep kids busy during their formative years. We did not have computers, telephones, electronic games or any other of the many devices kids have today. Some of the things we did as kids included the following:

We had the Port Theatre which provided us with double feature movies and cartoons on Saturdays. During the week, the theatre would show other types of movies including dramas, horror movies and documentaries. Kids could go to the movies on Saturday for an admission price of 9 cents. For a quarter, you could buy a ticket, get a bag of popcorn, a coke and have one penny left over.

I remember growing up knowing that Roy Rogers, Hop-a-long Cassidy and many others had cleaned up the West and that there was no more crime in the US. We certainly didn't have any crime in St. Joe. People didn't lock their homes or their cars in those days. I had a rude awakening when I got older.

For those who had cars or families with cars could go to the Bay View Drive-in Theatre, which was located just across the Highland View Bridge, approximately where Raffield Fisheries is now located. Movies would begin about dust dark and last for two or three hours.

Also, those kids with their own cars or who would be able to borrow the family car would be known to "drag" Reid Avenue especially on Friday and Saturday nights. Those who didn't have a car or didn't ride with their friends would stand on the sidewalk and wave to those who did. The big thing in those days was to see or be seen. When not "dragging" Reid, you may be seen at the White Spot Drive-in Restaurant or maybe Ms. Mary's Bay View Drive-in Restaurant, which later became Faye's (Gardner) Drive-in Restaurant. Later years introduced us to Sally's (Redd) Drive-in Restaurant.

We used to go to the city's baseball park which was located on Ave A, just past the AN Railroad Tracks. We would watch the "St. Joe Saints" Baseball Team play city town teams like Panama City, Apalachicola and other city leagues close by. The Centennial Baseball Park was later built at its present location and the city leagues continued to play for many years. High school football games would also be played in the outfield of this stadium since there was not a high school stadium at that time. Temporary bleachers would be set up during football season. Basketball games would be played at the Centennial Building also having temporary bleachers erected during the season.

In later years, after the high school gymnasium was built, the school would allow the high school kids to have dances and "sock hops" after the football and basketball games. There was a juke box located in the concession area of the gym and we would be allowed to play music and dance during the school lunch hour periods. Many kids learned to do the Panama City Bop and other dances such as the Shag and the Twist.

The STAC House was first located in the American Legion Building on Third Street, across from Rich's IGA. The City eventually built a new building on Eighth Street just off of Woodward Avenue. I was on the committee selected to name our center. STAC stood for Sharks Teenage Center. There has always been some controversy concerning what STAC was derived from, but I can assure you that I was there, and I know for sure. Many kids have enjoyed this facility for more than sixty (60) years.

Part Two of this story to follow......

CHAPTER 41

KIDS GROWING UP IN PORT ST. JOE, FL - PART TWO

This is Part Two of a three-part story of kids growing up in Port St. Joe, Florida during the 1940's, 1950' and 1960's.

As stated in Part One, Port St. Joe had a lot to offer kids as they grew up there. Because of the natural resources surrounding our fair city, boys and girls were afforded many opportunities to have fun and fun is what we had.

So much could be said about beautiful St. Joseph Bay. We swam at the city pier, picked up scallops, went crabbing, cast netting, fishing and some even learned to water ski. Boy Scouts camped out on the shoreline, hiked to Cape San Blas and the list goes on.

We also swam, and water skied in the Bay, the Gulf, and the Highland View and White City Canals. There was hunting in the vast woodland areas and fishing on the rivers and lakes. During the summers, we had summer recreation programs sponsored by the city in conjunction with the school system. Many activities were enjoyed by those who chose to attend.

The Boy Scouts played an important role in shaping young lives in PSJ. I remember having soap box races on Palm Blvd. With the help of older Scouts and parents, soap box racing cars were built and raced. Small boys would ride in and steer the cars while larger boys would push. A lot of proud moments and some disappointments. No participation trophies were ever given, only trophies for the winners.

Speaking of the Scouts, there was a Boy Scout Troop, a Girl Scout Troop, Cub Scouts and Brownie Scouts. In 1955, the Boy Scout Troop was taken on a charted bus trip to Washington DC and New York City. While in Washington, we toured The Capitol, the Smithsonian Institute, and the FBI Building. We had our picture taken with Congressmen and Senators and we were presented an American Flag that had flown over the Capitol Building. In New York City, we visited the Empire State Building, went on a tour of Ellis island and the Statue of Liberty. Quite a trip for us boys, some of who had never been on the other side of Wewa.

On the beaches, we went fishing, boating, swimming, water skiing, carpet golfing, roller skating, horseback riding, dancing at the Patio and at the Surf Restaurant Patio which was right down on the beach. Also, at Mexico Beach, there was a fishing pier which had a restaurant with a lighted dance floor and several motel rooms. The pier was owned by Mr. George Tapper and was named The Piertel. It weathered several storms and was eventually destroyed beyond repair by a hurricane.

In later years we also had a skating rink in Oak Gove. Also, in Oak Grove, was the famed Stripling's Community Store which later became Swan's Community Store. Most PSJ High students were totally familiar with this landmark.

Port St. Joe also had its own bowling alley, which was named St. Joe Bowling Lanes.

Part Three of this three-part story to be continued........

CHAPTER 42

KIDS GROWING UP IN PORT ST. JOE, FL - PART THREE

This is Part Three of a three-part story about kids growing up in Port St. joe, Florida during the 1940's, 1950's and 1960's.

As we got older, some of us kids were lucky or unlucky enough to have small motorized scooters and motorcycles. We must have ridden and explored close to a million miles over all the dirt roads in Port St. Joe and Gulf county (well maybe not quite a million miles). We would also tie old car hoods up-side-down on a rope to the back of a jeep or a Model A Ford and pull one another on the hoods down the beach. The hoods would get hot and we would run the vehicle out into shallow water so that the hood could cool off. We also took Jeeps to Cape San Blas and road on the beach as well as up and down the sand dunes. At that time, there were no houses or roads on the Cape and there were no laws against riding on the beach or the dunes. We sure had some good times over there.

When some of us got older, we raced our speed boats in the bay and in the canals. We also drag raced our cars on the Ward Ridge Road, Jones Homestead Road and on the Simmons Bayou Road. Back in the day, there weren't too many cars traveling on these roads and we were lucky enough to do these stupid things without mishap or being caught by the Law.

Speaking of the Law, we were protected by the Port St. Joe Police Department, the Gulf County Sheriff's Department and the Local Florida Highway Patrol. Chief Buck Griffin and his City Patrolmen, Murdock Kelly, Howard Rogers and Barney Fife. Yes, we had our own Barney. Sheriff's Officers, Wayne White and Jimmy Barfield. Florida Highway Patrolman Ken Murphy. All of these officers were friends of our parents and were our friends as well. Back in the day, everyone knew everyone else and you did your best not to get into trouble.

I don't know how we did all that racing without ever being caught.

Last but not least, Port St. Joe Parents were God fearing people and believed that their kids should attend Sunday School and Church. Most of them saw to it that we attended regularly and that we were taught the difference between right and wrong. I have a confession to make. I didn't always give the Lord his offering like my mother taught me to do but in my adult life, I think I have made up for it.

We kids lived in the best home town in America, Port St. Joe, Florida.

CHAPTER 43

GRANDADDY'S FELT HAT

Many years ago, in Port St. Joe, Florida, my Granddaddy, (T.H. Stone) had two (2) felt hats. Granddaddy was affectionately called "Uncle Hig" by many of his friends. One of his hats was his Sunday-go-to-meeting hat, and the other one was his everyday hat. Now.... every morning except Sunday, he would put on his everyday hat and walk from his house on Hwy 98 downtown to Honey's Café. He would buy a newspaper and a cup of coffee, many times served by Honey's son, Ferrel Allen. Ferrel was a young teen at that time and often helped his mother in the café.

Now my grandmother (Mama Stone) hated Granddaddy's everyday hat. This was an old hat that he had worn for years and it had certainly seen better times. He wore it when working on his old houses, working in his garden and it had surely earned the name of "everyday hat". It was stained, frayed and also had some small holes in it for some unknown reason. Mama Stone would say on many occasions, "Hig, you need to throw that old hat away and get you another one." He would reply, "Nope, this one suits me just fine."

One Saturday, when Granddaddy was taking a bath, Mama Stone took the old hat and threw it in the garbage can and remarked, "He'll have to get him a new hat now." Well....that wasn't the end of this story. When Granddaddy got dressed and couldn't find his hat, he immediately hollered out, "Mrs. Stone, where's my hat?" Mama Stone said, "Hig, I've been asking you for a long time now to get rid of that old hat and you wouldn't hear of it, so I took it upon myself to dispose of it myself." "What do you mean, you disposed of it Woman?" He replied, "That was my favorite hat." She then explained, "I threw that nasty thing in the garbage where it belongs." Now...Granddaddy wasn't at all amused at what she had done and immediately went to the garbage can to retrieve his old "everyday" hat. Being in the garbage can for a while certainly didn't help the smell of that old hat so he went into the kitchen and washed it with lye soap, rinsed it out and put it on the back-door steps to dry. Mama Stone wasn't very happy with him about this but knew she had lost that battle.

Later that day, when Mama Stone was in the kitchen cooking, Granddaddy went into her closet and took five of her best and newest hats and went outside and threw them all into the middle of Hwy 98. Just as he threw the last one in the road, Mama Stone came to the door and hollowed, "Hig, what in the world are you doing?" Granddaddy replied, "Just making sure you don't get any more ideas about throwing away my favorite hat again." Mama Stone was able to save three of the five hats from being run over by automobiles. My mother said that Mama Stone never spoke of Granddaddy's old "everyday" hat again.

The picture is of my granddaddy wearing the old everyday hat while having coffee at Honey's Café.

CHAPTER 44

GOING ON STRIKE...
A ONE MAN STRIKE...
5 CENTS AN HOUR

Back in about 1960 Mr. Edgar Strange worked on the Line Crew for St. Joseph Telephone and Telegraph Company. As customary each work-day morning, Mr. Strange would always drive the line truck out of the fenced-in area and park it in front of the small telephone warehouse so that it could be loaded with the necessary telephone apparatus needed for work each day.

On one particular morning, Edgar parked the truck and got out and went into the warehouse and sat down on a nail keg. When Uncle Sec Singletary, who was the Line Crew Foreman, saw Edgar sitting down, he hollered, "Get up and go load the truck, Edgar." Edgar replied, "I'll not do it Son-Man, I'm going on strike and I'm waiting on the Man." The "Man" he was referring to was Mr. Joe Sharit, who was the Vice-President and General Manager of the Telephone Company at the time.

Now since Edgar was on strike, the rest of the crew had to just sit and wait for Mr. Sharit to arrive also. They all sat there from 7:00 until almost 8:15. About that time, Mr. Sharit was pulling into his parking place in front of his office at the railroad building next door and spotted the line truck still sitting in front of the warehouse. He promptly drove on down to see why that truck was still there when it clearly should have been gone by 7:30.

93

As Mr. Sharit exited his car, he said to Uncle Sec, "What's going on here? What's that truck still doing here at this time of morning and why are these men just sitting around?" Uncle Sec replied, "It's Edgar, Mr. Sharit. He says he's going on strike." Mr. Sharit then said to Edgar, "What do you mean Edgar, that you're going on strike?" Edgar quickly spoke up and said, "That's right Mr. Sharit. I'm going on strike. I want a nickel an hour raise." "You got it.." Mr. Sharit quipped back. "Now get on that truck and go to work."

As far as I know, that was the only strike ever against St. Joseph Telephone and Telegraph company and it was certainly the shortest.

CHAPTER 45

40 DEGREES & THE TOP DOWN

In the winter of 1961, Mr. Bert Munn Sr. went to Panama City one day. The purpose of the trip was to purchase a new family car, however, no one in the family knew anything about it. It was to be a surprise. Now Mr. Bert, being very dapper, was all dressed up in a suit, also wearing a top coat and a felt hat.

Mr. Bert drove all over Panama City visiting several new car dealerships before deciding just which car he would buy. After being gone for several hours, Mr. Munn finally returned home driving a new 1961 Dodge Convertible.

When Ms. Ocille came out to see the car, Mr. Bert was sitting there in the car with the top down, with his overcoat and hat on. After showing her the car, Ms. Ocille, noting that it was about 40 degrees, said, "Bert, what in the world are you doing with the top down, with it being so cold?" Mr. Bert said, "Well when I bought the car, the top was down and being excited about the new car and everything I just drove off without asking how to put it up."

CHAPTER 46

THE SOUTH BOUND ADVENTURE TO & FROM TARPON SPRINGS

Back in 1961, I purchased this 1953 Chevrolet Convertible from Robert Nedley. Shortly thereafter, my friend Michael Munn and I decided to travel down to Tarpon Springs to visit with one of our other friends, Abe Miller. Abe was working down there with Vitro and invited us to come stay with him until we could find a job.

When we were ready to leave St. Joe, it was a beautiful Spring day, so we put the top down, loaded our bags, told our families goodbye and took to the road. When we reached Perry, I remember commenting that this was the first time either of us had ever been out town by ourselves. What a time we would have, being out in the world on our own. We were excited.

Several hours later, we finally rolled into Tarpon Springs and found our way to Abe's apartment. Abe was glad to see someone from home and began showing us around. The plan was to get up early the next morning and head over to Tampa to start looking for a job.

So far, things were going pretty much as planned. We got up, had breakfast and started the trip to Tampa. Once in Tampa, we bought a local newspaper and began to search the want ads for a job. Mike found an interesting ad with little information but the promise of a good opportunity. We found a payphone and placed a call to inquire about the job(s). We were given directions to an office in downtown Tampa and were soon on our way to an interview. We were interviewed separately and were both accepted as possible employees of a company that was reluctant to explain what we would be doing. We thought that to be a little strange but decided to hang in there for the initial training that would start right after lunch. We were instructed to meet at a certain restaurant for lunch where we learned that several other young guys would also be training for the same type job.

The first order of business was to have lunch and then we would be paired up with a Trainer. Almost everyone ordered steaks but Mike and me. We knew we had to conserve our money, so we both ordered a hamburger. Turned out that the Company was paying for everybody's lunch.

After lunch, we were each assigned to a separate Trainer and rode with him out to a residential area, parked the car and began knocking on doors. Most people weren't home, and others didn't want to be bothered but the Trainer finally talked a lady into letting us inside where he began his "spill". Turned out that we were there to sell encyclopedias and it only took me about 3 minutes to figure out that it was not in any way something that I was remotely interested in doing. That lady must have figured it wasn't something she was interested in either because in less than 5 minutes we were asked to leave.

Once outside and headed for the next house, I quickly realized that I needed to go to the restroom. I told the Trainer that I would meet him at the next intersection after I found "facilities". The next intersection just happened to be a main highway that lead to downtown Tampa. It wasn't long before I was on a city bus that took me back to within two blocks of where we left my car.

Now Old Mike must not have needed to use the restroom quite as bad as I did because I waited until almost dark for him to finally reach the car. Turned out that he wasn't as lucky as I was in catching that bus and he had to walk all the way back to the downtown area. We quickly headed back to Tarpon Springs to Abe's place. The next morning, we gave Abe some reason as to why we had to return to Port St. Joe. Truth was, we were already homesick, and we soon turned that old Chevy North and away we came back to where we started from. We were home at the end of the third day.

We still laugh about this experience. Thanks for the memories, Mike.

CHAPTER 47

HIGH FINANCE

This is a story about high finance experiences at Florida National Bank in Port St. Joe, Apalachicola State Bank in Apalachicola and Wewahitchka State Bank in Wewahitchka.

Many years ago, in about 1961, my dad told me that I should begin establishing a good credit rating. He offered to take me down to Florida National Bank in Port St. Joe and co-sign a note for $200. The plan was to put the money in a checking account and to make monthly payments until it was paid in full. This seemed like a good thing to do, so I went with him to the bank where he introduced me to the President, Mr. Barke. Mr. Barke agreed to make the loan. Things went as planned and soon I paid off the loan being proud that I now had credit with this bank.

Shortly after paying off the Florida Bank loan, I decided to venture out to another bank which took me down to the Apalachicola State Bank in Apalachicola. When I went inside, I asked to see the President and after a few minutes, Mr. Rodman Porter came out of his office and said, "Young man, may I help you?" I said, "Yes sir, my name is Higdon Swatts, I'm from Port St. Joe and I would like to borrow $200 from your bank." He said, "Well, come on into my office."

Once inside, he asked "Do you know Ralph Swatts?" I said, "Yes Sir, I know two of them. One's my daddy and one's my brother." Mr. Porter replied, "Then that would make Maybel Stone Swatts your mother, right?" I said. "Yes Sir." He then added, "And that would make Mr. Hig Stone your grandfather, right?" I replied,

"Yes Sir." Mr. Porter then asked, "How much did you say you want to borrow?" Right away, I said "$500." Mr. Porter signaled for Jimmy Philyaw, who was the Head Cashier, to come in to his office. He then said to Jimmy, "Fix this boy up with whatever he wants." I left the bank with $300 more than I had planned to borrow and paid it back in about six months thus establishing credit with a second bank.

Now a year or so later, I also established credit with the Wewahitchka State Bank in Wewahitchka. One day I decided to go up to Blountstown, to buy an old car for $600. I only had $400, so I stopped by the Wewa Bank on the way, to borrow the other $200. Mr. Kenneth Whitfield was the Head Cashier, so I approached him about the loan.

He said, "Higdon, I'm sorry, but we have loaned out the maximum amount by law that we are allowed to loan against our deposits and we will have to wait until we get some paid back, before we can make any more loans." I then said "Well Kenneth, I didn't know ya'll were in such bad shape. I've got $400 out in the car, if you think that'll do ya'll some good." Kenneth didn't think that was too funny, anyway I found out later that the old car had already been sold.

That's my story about high finance and the above three banks.

CHAPTER 48

THE "GRIT NEWSPAPER" & THE "THINKING MACHINE"

In 1962, when I started working for the Telephone Company, I worked in the little small red brick Telephone Company building on First Street. This building was located right next to the A.N. Railroad parking lot and has since been torn down. It was the site of the Telephone Company Warehouse. I was hired to answer the telephone for Mr. E.J. Baxley, who was the Outside Plant Supervisor. This being somewhat of a boring job, I soon talked Mr. Baxley into letting me order telephone apparatus used for the installation of telephones.

Right inside the front door was a Western Union Teleprinter, which was used to receive service orders for long line telephone service between our company and Southern Bell Telephone Company in Panama City. As was often the case, this teleprinter would print what we called "garbage" whenever there was trouble on the telephone line. The "garbage" looked something like this, !@#$%^&* (Sometimes a whole page or two at a time).

Late one Friday afternoon, a little boy about 10 years old, came in the door and said, "Hey Mister, do you want to buy a Grit Paper?" About that time, that teleprinter started printing a page full of "garbage" and the little boy turned and looked at the machine and said, "Whut's dat thing?" I replied that, "It's a thinking machine."

"A Whut?" he asked and I said, "It's a thinking machine." He then said "Well whut do it think?" I then said that, "You have to ask it a question and it will answer you." I heard him ask a question but the teleprinter remained silent. He then said, "Hit didn't say nuttin". I then replied that, "You have to get down close to the keyboard and then ask the question."

He leaned over the keyboard again and said, "Who invented the Cotton Gin?" All of a sudden, that teleprinter began printing out the most "garbage" that I'd ever seen (about two pages). The little boy looked at the printed "garbage" on the paper and asked, "Whut's it thinking?" I walked around from behind the counter and tore the paper off the teleprinter, studied the pages for about a minute and then said, "Looks like to me it says, Eli Whitney."

About that time, his eyes got big, he dropped the bundle of Grit Papers and took off running out the door and away he went. About 15 minutes later, he returned with 5 more little boys, all wanting to see that "Thinking Machine".

It was the devil that made me do it.

CHAPTER 49

A $35 CHECK FOR THE SHERIFF'S WIFE"

In the summer of 1962, a bunch (7) of us St. Joe boys were "attending" National Guard Training Camp in a wooded area near Hinesville, Georgia. Most of us had never been past Wewahitchka and much less all the way to Georgia. It was during this time that my friend, Ed Bobbitt and I, both about 21 years of age, began to make more serious plans to make a trip the to the big city of Atlanta. It was decided that we would go a couple of weeks after returning from "camp".

Two weeks after returning, we finalized our plans, which included packing a small bag, filling up with gas and deciding that we would leave on Friday afternoon after work. We did not know where we would stay or what we would do when we got there. I don't even remember if we talked about that or not.

Well, the Friday of two weeks later finally came and after leaving work that day, we were off to Atlanta in my little Austin Healey. We put the top down just to be cool. It was somewhere around 8:00PM when we tooled through the little town of Newton, GA. Just after leaving the city limits, we came up behind a black 1954 two door Ford, doing about 45 mph. Now the Georgia speed limit in those days was 55 during the day and 50 after dark. Not wanting to drive 45 all the way to Atlanta, I decided to go around that Ford and in doing so, I managed to get the little Healey up to about 55 and went around that slowpoke.

Just as we got back into the right lane, the man driving that old Ford turned on a red light and pulled us over. When he approached our car, he identified himself as the Constable of Baker County and asked to see my driver's license. He then instructed us to follow him back to the county court house jail (see picture below) which was in the big city of Newton, population of 387 people.

At that time, he turned us (me) over to the Deputy Sheriff on duty and explained to him what I was charged with doing. The Deputy said that he would have to call the Justice of The Peace and tell him of the charges.

Once he had done that, the honorable one on the other end of the phone, asked to speak with me. Once on the phone, he said "Son, are you guilty?" and I replied, "Well I had to get up to 55mph to get around that Constable." And he then said, "You're guilty and the fine is $35." He then asked to speak to the Deputy again and when the Deputy hung up, he said "that'll be $35 for the fine."

Now $35 was a lot money in 1962 and I knew if I paid that amount in cash, that we would most likely have to turn around and go back to Port St. Joe because that would really cut into my spending money for the trip on to Atlanta. I then looked over at Ed and he had this look on his face as if to say, don't look at me, I don't have any extra money.

I then asked the Deputy if he could take a check and barely got the words out of my mouth, when he said, "No siree." It was then that I asked him if he would let me call the Sheriff of Gulf County to get verification that my check would be good. He said that if my sheriff said it would be good, then he would accept my check.

Now knowing that the Sheriff of Gulf County would most likely not be at the sheriff's office this late, I had to devise a backup plan just in case. When I called the sheriff's office, Edward Kay, who was the Jailer answered. Now I had known Edward for a number of years, so I said "Sheriff, this is Higdon" and proceeded to explain to him what I needed. He then replied, "Let me talk to the Deputy." When the Deputy hung up, he said, "That sheriff must think a lot of you. He said that whatever the amount of the check you wrote, that it would be good." The Deputy had me write the check to the sheriff of Baker County.

Ole Ed (Young Ed back then) and I got back on the road to Atlanta and for the life of me, I can't remember what we did after getting there. After returning to Port St. Joe, I do remember a few weeks later receiving my cancelled check back from my bank and it had been cashed at a Newton grocery store and endorsed by the wife of the sheriff.

CHAPTER 50

THE SINGING TELEGRAM

Many folks who lived in Port St. Joe back in the day, remember that the Telephone Company once provided Telegraph Service. Telegrams were received in the office, prepared for delivery and then delivered by a messenger. As technology progressed, telegrams eventually became a thing of the past.

There was one story though, that comes to mind about a telegram that was dispatched to be delivered to a certain lady in town. Now the messenger at that time was a man named "Cat" Sylvester. (I'm not sure if anyone ever knew what Cat's real name was but Cat was the name he was known by).

On this particular day, Cat boarded his three-wheel Cushman Motor Scooter and proceeded to the lady's house on 13th Street. When he arrived, he walked up on her front porch and rang her door-bell. When the lady came to the door, Cat told her he had a telegram for her. The lady asked, "Is it a singing telegram?" Cat said, "No Ma'am, it's just a regular telegram." She then said "Oh....I was hoping it was a singing telegram. All my life, I have wished for a singing telegram. Would you please sing it to me?"

Now Old Cat had never been asked to sing a telegram before and he quickly replied that he couldn't sing but before he could finish getting it out of his mouth, the lady interrupted him and just insisted that he sing her the telegram. Old Cat said that he would give it a try and began opening the envelope containing the telegram.

He then began tapping his foot on the wooden porch floor and began to sing, "Dah dah ta dah dah dah, Your sister Rose is dead."

CHAPTER 51

THE FROG STRANGLER &
THE HOLLOW LOG

One day in the Spring of 1965, I hooked up my boat and headed to Depot Creek. After I launched the boat, I decided to run up to Lake Wimaco to catch a mess of fish. I guess I had fished about all afternoon when I decided to start back. Just as I reached the mouth of the Canal, dark clouds soon loomed over me and it wasn't long before I was in the worst frog strangler of a downpour that I had ever been in. Of course, I didn't have any rain gear with me and I was soon getting pelted to the point it weren't no fun. (Pardon the English, I know better, but I don't care at this point in my life).

I got to thinking that I'd best pull over to the bank of the canal and seek shelter under a big Cypress tree. It rained so hard that even under that tree, I was about to drown. I spotted a hollow log laying on the ground, just big enough for me to crawl in. I soon found my myself finally safe (I thought) snuggled up inside that log.

After about 45 minutes, the rain stopped, and I thought I might better get started back to the landing. As I tried to wiggle my way out, I soon realized I was stuck. No matter how hard I tried, I just couldn't free myself. By this time, it was beginning to get dark and being stuck in a hollow log at dark thirty wasn't something that I was very happy about.

Soon, I began to think about the possibility of other "critters" crawling up in that log with me and to say the least I was getting scared. Being scared is one thing but being scared while inside a log with the thought of a critter being in there with me was something else.

Someone once told me that if you were scared, that you need to start thinking about something else, in other words, get your mind off of being scared. I decided it might help, so I started to think about politics. I began to think about the last national election and that it had been the first one I had ever voted in. I remembered that I had voted Democrat and had voted for Lyndon Johnson.

Taking a moment to reflect on that, made me feel so small, that I just crawled right out of that log. I was soon on my way home. Haven't voted for a Democrat since.

CHAPTER 52

NEVER COUNT YOUR MONEY UNTIL IT'S IN THE PALM OF YOUR HAND

Back in 1965, when I was 23 years old, I spent a few months selling cars for my brother at Jim Cooper Chevrolet-Pontiac & Oldsmobile Company in Port St. Joe. One day, Mr. Walter Stafford from White City drove into town and wanted to look at new cars. Mr. Stafford was interested in trading his wife's 1960 Pontiac in for a new 1965 Pontiac Bonneville. He soon decided on the car he liked and wanted to know how we could trade. I told him I would have to get his old car appraised so that I would be able quote him on the trade difference. He agreed and shortly I returned and handed him a written quote. He looked at it hurriedly and seemed pleased with the price but wanted to know if he could take the car out to show his wife. Of course, I agreed, and he soon left with the car.

Now while Mr. Stafford was gone, I began to think about the $300 commission I was going to make on this sale and even thought about what I would do with it. I would be able to pay my car payment, my car insurance premium and even pay my gas bill at Mr. Frank Pates Shell Station.

In about an hour, Mr. Stafford returned, saying that his wife loved the car and that he was ready to make the trade. I asked him to sit down with me in the office so that I could write up the deal. Soon, I handed him the paperwork ready for his signature. He took one look and said, "This is not what we agreed to." Being somewhat startled, I replied, "What do you mean?" He then proceeded to tell me that the total was more than I had quoted. I quickly explained to him that the only difference was that I had added in the sales tax and tag transfer. This amount had been quoted in the original written quote but all he had focused on was the amount of the trade difference. At that point, Mr. Stafford got up and said he wasn't going to pay any more than the trade difference. He then left the office and drove away in his wife's old car. Needless to say, I was very upset. In my mind, I had already been paid that commission and paid those bills with money I had yet to receive. The rest of my day was not good.

Late that afternoon, Mr. Stafford returned to the dealership with his wife. She said that she had come with him to make sure that he didn't make another excuse for not buying her that car. She added, "I told him he was crazy to think y'all would sell him that car without collecting sales tax. So, we are here to pay for my new car, including the sales tax and tag." I replied, "Yes Ma'am."

Soon after the Stafford's had left with their new car, I began to think about the fact that you can't count your money until it's laying in the palm of your hand and that you certainly can't spend it either. This was a lesson that I never forgot.

CHAPTER 53

NEVER JUDGE ANYONE BY THEIR LOOKS

This story is related to a recent story I told about, when I sold cars for Jim Cooper Chevrolet in Port St. Joe during the mid 1960's. There was an elderly gentleman from Apalachicola that came in wanting to purchase a new car. He was driving an old 1959 Chevrolet Station Wagon. He got out of his car and began looking at new Impala's. Three of the other salesmen began talking about the man's dirty clothes and making remarks like, "Look at that old man. he don't look like he can afford to buy anything". While they continued to talk about the old fella, I quickly made my way out to greet him and asked if there was any way I could help him. As it turned out, the man bought a new car from me and paid cash for it. I later found out that he was one of the richest men in Apalachicola.

A month or two later, a local man started showing up at the dealership around lunch time every day for about two weeks. Each day I would go out to greet him and I learned that he was planning to buy a car just as soon as he could get his credit union loan approved. The other salesmen would ask me why I wasted my time waiting on this guy every day and I would just say to them that one day he might just come back in and buy a car.

The third week, the local man came in, asked for me, purchased and paid cash for the car that he had been looking at.

The title of this story says it all.

CHAPTER 54

TRIP TO ATLANTA
– 1955 CHEVROLET

On one brisk January morning back in 1967, I left Port St. Joe headed to Panama City to catch a Southern Airways DC3 one-way to Atlanta, Georgia. The purpose of the trip was to find and purchase a 1955 Chevrolet. Now the 1955 Chevrolet was just about my favorite automobile of all time and I was hoping to be able to purchase a car for around $700.

Yes, you read that right, $700. Twelve-year-old cars at that time were pretty cheap in comparison to the prices of today's cars. I had the $700 in my wallet along with another $200 hidden in another compartment. I was planning to buy a car for $700 and have the extra $200 for expenses. I had to get back to Port St. Joe, and I figured that $200 would be enough.

The plan was to fly to Atlanta, rent a car and drive up and down the streets of that fair city, visiting all the used car lots and hopefully find the car of my dreams. I got a little excited when the old DC3 touched down in Atlanta and I was allowed to deplane. I believe that this was only the second time that I had flown in an airplane and both times it was to Atlanta.

Following my plan, I proceeded to the Hertz Rental Car Agency located in airport terminal. The rental car just happened to be a brand new 1967 Red Ford Galaxie XL and I thought at least I would be riding in style, while looking for my '55 Chevy.

Even in 1967, Atlanta was a mighty big city, especially for an old Port St. joe boy who had never been past Wewa but a time or two. I left the airport and drove around until I finally found what was called Used Car Alley.

After about two hours, I spotted a black 1955 Bel Air Chevy and quickly pulled into the car lot to look. It didn't take me long to look that car over because it looked like it had been wrecked, warmed over and put out next to the curve just to get my attention. Just as I had decided that this was not the car for me, a salesman dressed in a zoot suit approached me wanting to sell me the car. I explained to him that I wasn't interested and started to get back in the rental car when I spotted another '55 parked up next to the office.

When asking about that one, the salesman said that it belonged to him and that it was not for sale. He then told me all about the car. He had just had it painted resale red, put new American Mag wheels on it with new tires, installed a new 327 engine with a Muncie 4-speed transmission as well as new white pleated seats. I then asked that if he were to sell it, what would be the asking price. He thought for a minute and said that he might consider selling it for around $1400.

I then proceeded to tell him that I only had $700 and that I would just have to keep looking. "Would you give $1200 for it?" he asked. I replied that I probably would if I had it but that I only had $700. "Well" he said, "I would never take $700 for it." I told him I understood and then starting walking toward the rental car.

Once again, he spoke up asking, "Would you pay $1000 for it?" I replied once again that I would if I had it but $700 was all that I had. "Alright" he said, "I'll let you have it for $700." Being surprised, I told him that I would take it and we began walking toward the office. All of a sudden, he said "Ain't no way I 'm selling you that car for $700."

Being a little bit irritated, I turned and headed back toward the rental car explaining that I didn't have any more time to waste and if I was going to find a car, I needed to get on with it. As I backed up to turn around, here he comes again saying that he would sell it to me. "Are you sure?" I asked. He said yes, and we went into the office where he wrote up the Bill of Sale and the receipt. Once it was paid for, I locked it up, drove the rental car back to the airport, checked it in and caught a taxi back to the car lot to pick up the '55.

I spent one night and left early the next morning heading back to Port St. Joe driving the car of my dreams. Never would I have expected to buy such a nice car for just $700.

CHAPTER 55

FIVE DOLLARS DOWN & FIVE DOLLARS A MONTH

Some of you from Port St. Joe will remember Roche's Furniture Store downtown. Mr. Weldon Roche, the owner, was a fine gentleman who dabbled a little bit in local politics and once served as a Gulf County Commissioner.

One day in 1968, I just happened to pass by his store and decided to go in and take a look around. While I was browsing, Mr. Roche spotted me looking at a dining room set and said to me, "Why don't you buy that, it's on sale for 50% off." I told him that I really couldn't afford it. He then replied, "You don't need any money, you can just pay for it anyway you want to." Well....that kinda got my attention, so I said, "You mean that?" He said, "Yes, your credit is good with me."

Now... the devil in me cranked up and said, "Well how about I pay you $5.00 down and $5.00 a month until it's paid off." I really don't think he expected me to say that because he began staring at that old tile floor with a frown on his face. He finally looked up at me and said, "If that's what you want to do, then it's alright with me." We then meandered to the back of the store where he wrote up the charge ticket and I gave him the down payment of $5.00.

Now I never expected him to wait on his money forever, but I thought I would have a little fun at his expense. I had the money to pay for the furniture right then, but I didn't want him to know it. I waited about 30 days before I went back in his store and purposely waited until he was through waiting on another customer. I then told him I was ready to make my first $5.00 payment.

He looked a little annoyed but began writing up the receipt. While he was writing, I said to him, "While you're at it, how about telling what my balance is." He looked up at me as if he could have killed me and said, "IT'S $5.00 LESS THAN IT WAS A MONTH AGO." I thanked him and then said, "If you don't mind, go ahead and make that receipt for the full amount of the balance."

You should have seen the relief on his face when he realized he was getting all of his money at once. I often wondered if he ever made that deal to any other customer to let them pay whenever they wanted to. I kinda felt bad about what I did but not really bad. It was fun to see the looks he gave me. I was just taking care of "business" as I was known to do.

CHAPTER 56

UNBELIEVABLE GAS MILEAGE

Back in the 1960's, Nissan Motor Company began importing Datsun cars and trucks into the US. One certain gentleman, who worked for St. Joe Paper Company, purchased a new Datsun pickup truck. He was so proud of his new truck and began telling his fellow workers at the Mill all about it. For weeks on end, he would brag about the great gas mileage the truck was getting and that the more miles he put on the truck, the better the mileage became. After hearing about this almost every day, his co-workers decided to play a trick on their friend.

One day after the truck owner had clocked in, they slipped out to the parking lot and added a gallon of gas in the little truck's gas tank. A few days later, the gentleman, once again, began bragging about the great gas mileage the truck was getting. The co-workers added gas to the truck's tank several more times without him knowing what was going on and the bragging continued. Then, all of a sudden, the bragging ceased, and the owner of the truck didn't even mention the truck for about two weeks.

One of the co-workers asked the gentleman why he never talked about his truck's mileage anymore. He said, "Well, the gas mileage went from about 23 miles per gallon to 45 miles per gallon and I felt like no one would believe that it could do that well, so I decided it was best not say anything more about it. Then, when I checked the mileage last week, it was only getting 23 miles per gallon and now I just don't know what to think, but you better

119

believe that I will be telling that Datsun Dealer a thing or two when I take it in for service next week."

It is not known by this writer if the co-workers ever admitted to their friend what they had done, but more than likely the subject never came up again.

CHAPTER 57

MY EARLY YEARS
ON CAPE SAN BLAS

In the early 1960's, my friends and I spent a lot of time on Cape San Blas. During those days, there were no roads, no houses and no State Park. There was only a two-rut sandy road that went from just past Vitro, just about all the way to the end of the Point. This road was mostly in the center of the peninsula with many sand dunes, pine trees, prickly pairs and other wild beach like plants being on either side. The unofficial name of that road was T.H. Stone Highway, named after my grandfather.

Mr. Fred Maddox owned a bunch of cows and a few hogs that roamed freely throughout the area. Most of the time when we went to the Cape, Mr. Fred could be seen coming or going in his old 1953 green Jeep pickup truck. I guess he would have been there checking on his livestock. I always had the feeling that Mr. Fred had other reasons to be on the Cape, but not saying I knew exactly what those reasons might have been.

You had to own a jeep, dune buggy or some sort of four (4) wheel-drive vehicle, to be able to travel on the Cape. Maybe you just had to be friends with someone else who owned a jeep to be able to have the fun of exploring one of Florida's last frontiers. Of course if you were lucky enough to own a boat, you could be on the Cape within minutes of the city boat basin in Port St. Joe.

In about 1964, when I was about 23 years old, I bought an old rusty Willys Jeep for two ($200.00) hundred dollars. Since I had to spend money on the jeep every time I went to the Cape, it wasn't long before I had eight ($800.00) hundred dollars in that old jeep that was still worth about two ($200.00) hundred dollars. Some of my friends also had old jeeps and we would all load up the jeeps with our friends, snacks and other "refreshments" making the journey to our favorite beach. We outfitted our jeeps with CB radios so when got separated, we could communicate our location to the others. Before each trip, we would stop by the Western Auto Associate store to stock up on ammunition for our "22" automatic firearms, so we could do our target practicing when we got to the Cape. It was nothing in those days to strap on our guns and holsters, drive the open top jeeps downtown and go into Dave May's store, which just happened to be right next door to the small Police Dept. Shack. The police apparently didn't think too much about it.

With three or four jeeps, all going in different directions, it was easy to get separated but eventually we would all meet up in order to tell some tall tales, eat and go swimming. Back in the day, there were no laws restricting you from riding up and down the dunes, nor riding on the beach. The dunes were very high and the jeeps would sometime slide down the slopes sideways. We had so much fun. During those days, we had never ever even heard of the term "endangered environment".

I remember on one excursion, my bother Ralph was riding "shotgun" with me in my jeep. All of a sudden, we spotted one of Mr. Fred's small calves running down the beach. Ralph hollered, "Speed up and get up side him." Being the obedient brother that he had taught me to be, I did just as he told me and soon my jeep and that calf were running side by side when Brother Ralph stood up and before I knew what was happening, he dove off of that jeep attempting to catch the calf around the neck in order to throw him down. Not only did he miss the calf, but the calf kicked him in the throat and down he went, head first into the white sandy beach. Thinking that he had probably broken his fool neck, I quickly spun around to go back and check on him. By the time I got back to him, he was getting up and spitting sand out of his mouth. I just knew he was really hurt, but do you think he would admit he was hurt? Nah. One thing for sure though, he never tried that stunt again.

There would be many more trips to the Cape, some of which no one ever spoke of again, but there are still the "memories".

CHAPTER 58

WOULD YOU SHUT YOUR DARN DOG UP

Now everyone knows that one of the things that dogs are supposed to do, is to bark when something strange is going on outside. It's called being a good Watchdog.

Port St. Joe certainly has always had its share of good Watchdogs. Westcott Circle is no exception. One Westcott Circle resident, who is well known by many who have lived in this fair city for many years is a lady by the name of Sue Phillips. Now Sue just happens to be one of those people who says what she means and means what she says, if you know what I mean.

One night in the early 1970's Sue's phone rang at approximately 2 o'clock AM. When Sue answered, she recognized the gentleman's voice on the other end as one of her neighbors from across the street. All he said was, "Would you shut your darn dog up?" He then abruptly hung up. You notice, that I didn't use the word damn because I don't think that's a very nice word to use but to be truthful, that's the word the neighbor had used.

Now Sue wasn't even a bit amused by that type of call, being that it was 2 o'clock in the morning and everything and especially since she DIDN'T even have a dog. Eventually, Sue finally went back to sleep.

The next night, before going to bed, Sue set her alarm clock to go off at 2 o'clock in the morning. At about 10:00 PM, she finally decided that it was time for her to go to bed. Sure enough, at exactly 2 AM, Sue's alarm goes off, awakening her as planned. Sue reaches for her telephone and dials her across the street neighbors phone number. After letting it ring a few times, a sleepy man's voice on the other end of the line answered, "Uh...hello."

Now Sue uses this opportunity to follow through with her plan, and hollows through the telephones transmitter, "BOW WOW, BOW WOW!" Sue then gently hangs up the receiver, rolls over and goes back to sleep. She has since reported that she has never received any more early morning phone calls from her gentleman neighbor from across the street.

CHAPTER 59

LONG RIDE FROM TALLAHASSEE TO PORT ST. JOE

Back during the Christmas Season of 1978, my boss, Mr. Bernard Pridgeon, was flying into Tallahassee and ask me to drive over from Port St. Joe to pick him up at the airport. I, of course said ok, he being my boss and everything. Being that it was just a few days before Christmas, I made plans to go a few hours early and go Christmas shopping in Tallahassee before his plane arrived.

Now you have to understand that I was just fresh divorced and that I had plans to buy gifts for not only for my family but my ex's family and all the employees who worked in my office. The total number of gifts was 48. Being a man, it didn't take but about two and a half hours to complete my shopping. The employees at Sears and J.C. Penny's were glad to get rid of me because all of the kids' gifts were large items and took forever to ring up and put in bags. When I finally got the car loaded, the trunk and back seat didn't have an inch of room to spare.

Well now, it was just about time for Mr. Pridgeon's plane to arrive, so I hurried on out to the airport to pick him up. When he got to the car and saw all those gifts piled up in the back seat, he said, "I guess you better open the trunk, cause I don't see anywhere in the back seat to put my bags." He wasn't very amused when I told him the trunk was full too.

It was a long ride from Tallahassee to Port St. Joe with two suitcases in the middle of the front seat, piled so high that I couldn't see through the rearview mirror and I don't think Mr. Pridgeon was a happy camper either. Oh well...

CHAPTER 60

YOUR BANANA PLEASE

Most people have always taken their telephone service for granted. Most people who know me, know that I worked for the Telephone Company for many years.

One year in the mid-seventy's we were expecting a storm to develop into a hurricane. I had been asked to assist the telephone operators since many of the operators had evacuated with their families. We were short-handed and those of us who stayed behind were assigned certain jobs to do in order to maintain a reasonable level of service.

The company had just recently converted to direct distance dial service and with this conversion, all one-party lines were given the ability to dial long distance without any operator assistance. It was called automatic number identification. This meant that each call made, could be billed automatically without an operator having to ask the customer for his telephone number. On the other hand, customers with two and four-party lines could dial their own long-distance calls, however, an operator would receive a signal, interrupt the call and ask the customer for their telephone number. The operator would then key in the number on a key pad and release the call for completion. This process was called Operator Number Identification and this procedure would allow the calls to be billed to the customer.

Jean McMillian was the Supervisor on duty and had assigned me to an operator position with instructions on how to handle

128

operator number identification type calls. All I had to do was plug into a lighted switchboard jack and just say "Your number please?" Then key in the number the customer gave and release the call. This seemed simple enough, so I began handling calls.

An hour or so later, Jean told us that she was going next door to the grocery store to get a few items to make us some sandwich's. She returned shortly and began making the sandwiches. Just as I was receiving a signal, Jean asked me if I wanted a banana sandwich. I plugged into that jack and said to the customer, "Your banana please?" The customer said, "What?" I quickly responded with "your number please?"

I thought Jean and the others that had heard what I had said would die laughing. Some of them have never let me forget it either.

CHAPTER 61

BE CAREFUL WHOSE BOOTS YOU TRY TO FILL

If you worked for St. Joseph Telephone Company, you could always count on something unexpected to happen or maybe being pranked by someone.

We were always having trouble with the toilets getting stopped up. Most of the time it would be caused by someone flushing a paper towel down the drain. One day Jimmy Stephens, who worked as our Utility Man, came to me to report once again that the ladies room toilet was stopped up and what he had found to be the problem with the drain. Since this seemed to be happening fairly frequently, I told Jimmy to order two (2) electric hand dryers, one for the men's room and one for the ladies' room.

The next week, Jimmy told me that the dryers had been received and asked me when I wanted him to install them. We decided that we would put out a notice to everyone who worked in the building and make temporary signs to be put on the doors so that when he got ready to install the one in the ladies' room, the women could use the men's room and vice versa. The installation was scheduled for the next day.

As planned, before Jimmy started the installation, the signs were changed, and the employees were reminded once again of the temporary change and the work began. Soon one of the female employees went into the designated ladies room to use it and while inside one of the stalls, a man came in to use the other toilet. All the female employee could see under the stall was a man's cowboy boot.

The "man" was actually Jean McMillian, who had borrowed Ronnie Bishop's boots, filled up a coke bottle with water and was slowly pouring the water into the toilet as if, well you get the picture, don't you? The female employee, whose name I won't mention, hollered, " Ronnie Bishop, you get yourself out of here."

I think some of the other women had quietly slipped into the restroom to witness the reaction. All of a sudden, all of them burst into laughter and the jig was up.

CHAPTER 62

PEOPLE ARE FUNNY

A few years ago, the Telephone company had a large cable job going on in the Blountstown Exchange and as a result of this job, the contractor brought in about twenty (20) empty cable reels to St. Joe and put them inside our fenced-in cable yard. Our Line Crew Supervisor, Howard Neel, asked me what we were going to do with all the old reels. I said to him, "Just put them outside the fence next to First Street and put a sign on them marking them free."

He put those reels out next to the road and a week later he told me they were all still there. I told him to change the sign to read "Do not mess with these reels." Within two (2) days, all of those reels were gone.

People are funny.

CHAPTER 63

MY 1976 CADILLAC LIMO

Funny story about this 1976 Cadillac Limo. Jack Medley and I were driving back from Longwood and decided to get off I-75 and travel on Hwy US 41 for a while. Coming through Ocala, I spotted this Limo for sale on a used car lot. I told Jack I was going to turn around and go back and buy it. He said, "Yeah right." Well, I went back and asked about the Caddy and was told they wanted $5,000.00 for it. I said to the salesman, "But you don't understand, I only want to pay $2,500.00 for it out the door, tax and tag included."

Of course, he said they couldn't do that, but he would call his boss at the downtown lot to find out what they would be willing to take. After about four (4) phone calls to his boss, I ended up leaving there, driving the Caddy and only paid $2,500.00 total. Jack was shaking his head. I'm not going to tell you what my wife said when I drove up to the house in this Limo.

CHAPTER 64

THE WAITRESS &THE $1 MILLION DOLLAR BILL

Back in about 1997, I stopped at a local restaurant about 1:30 in the afternoon to get a sandwich. Shortly after being served, the young lady who had served me came back over to my table and said, "Sir, I clock out at 2:00 and I was wondering if you would mind allowing me go ahead and close out your check before I leave." I said that would be fine because I knew she would be wanting her tip before she left. I reached into my billfold and handed her a fake $1,000,000.00 bill. She said, "I'll be right back with your change."

I guess she had not looked at the bill but shortly thereafter she returned with the bill and said, "Sir, do you have anything smaller than this?" I said I thought I might and immediately gave her enough money to cover the cost of my sandwich and included enough for a nice tip. I don't think she ever knew that the large bill was fake. Haven't tried to pass that bill to anyone else since.

CHAPTER 65

T.H. STONE MEMORIAL STATE PARK CELEBRATES 50 YEARS

T.H. Stone Memorial State Park was named after my grandfather (Terrell Higdon Stone) 50 years ago. On November 5, 2017, the park celebrated the 50th year anniversary of being a state park. My grandfather was a prominent community leader and owner of the land prior to it being designated as a state park. It was one of his dreams to one day see the property made into a park. He passed away over 60 years ago and never knew that his dream would eventually come true.

The park was built by the State of Florida and was completed in 1967. That same year, Ben C. Williams, State Representative for Bay and Gulf Counties filed Florida State House Bill 1162 naming the park T. H. Stone Memorial State Park. During this celebration park officials recognized descendants of the T.H. Stone family, previous managers, organizations, staff and volunteers who have supported the park over the last 50 years. There were two bands playing music, displays and fun family activities. The park is located at: 8899 Cape San Blas Road, Port St. Joe, Florida.

AUTHORS NOTE

Although most every one of these stories are true, two or three of them may be on the edge of fiction…. uh are in fact fiction; however, most of them are based on actual events which happened during the formative years of the author who grew up in the small Northwest Florida Gulf Coast town of Port St. Joe.

ABOUT THE AUTHOR

Higdon Swatts is a lover of local history, and the short stories that fill these pages are drawn from personal experiences as he came of age in the small coastal town of Port St. Joe, Florida.

A firm believer in the importance of documenting local lore for the benefit of family, friends and acquaintances, the author hopes this book will inspire you to reflect on your own life and share what you remember.

Higdon lives in Panama City, Florida, with his wife, Gayle, and has plenty of stories left to be told.

The Way I Remember It

Made in the USA
Columbia, SC
30 March 2021

35315856R00093